WE BRING YOU THIS REPORT

**with our perplexed sense that something is
terribly wrong on Earth and with our questions:**
What shall we do?

Will you devote yourself, in passing to the new millennium,
to learning how all 6 billion of us humans can live
peacefully, justly, and sustainably on the Earth?

Will you help us all dream a new dream?

Will you who are religious and spiritual leaders
work together . . . to develop a community of Earth's faith
traditions that is an example of the communication,
respect, cooperation, and good will needed among all nations
and peoples?

Will you lead the way to a planet-wide spiritual celebration
of Earth's entry into a new era? Will you bring every person,
every community, every faith tradition to the celebration,
bringing gifts on behalf of the whole community of life?

If you will, the original source of creative energy
will surely show us all a new future.

Then, with hope in our hearts, we can die in peace—
all 6 billion of us—to our immature, 20th century ways
of being and thinking.

We can cross the waters together.

And we can celebrate Earth's arrival in a new era
that will be remembered forever.

—Dr. GERALD O. BARNEY, *based on his Plenary Address
to the Parliament of the World's Religions, Chicago, 1993*

In memory of Adupa

THRESHOLD 2000

Critical Issues and Spiritual Values
for a Global Age

Gerald O. Barney

with Jane Blewett and Kristen R. Barney

MILLENNIUM INSTITUTE ~ Arlington

CoNexus Press ~ Grand Rapids

Published by:

Millennium Institute

A nonprofit organization promoting long-term integrated thinking
1117 North 19th Street, Suite 900
Arlington, VA 22209-1708   U.S.A.

and by

CoNexus Press
6264 Grand River Dr. NE
Ada, MI 49301 USA

Order additional copies through your bookstore, or contact CoNexus Press at the address above, or by calling toll-free 1-877-784-7779 (in North America) or 616-682-9022 world-wide. By mail, send US $13.95 plus $3.00 shipping & handling. Visa and Mastercard accepted.

Publisher's Cataloging-in-Publication
(Provided by Quality Books, Inc.)
Barney, Gerald O.
    Threshold 2000 : critical issues and spiritual values
    for a global age / Gerald O. Barney ; with Jane Blewett
    and Kristen R. Barney. -- 2nd ed.
      p. cm.
    Includes bibliographical references.
    ISBN: 0-9637897-3-2
    1. Human ecology--Religious aspects. 2. Human ecology
    --Forecasting. 3. Twenty-first century--Forecasts. 4.
    Religion and ethics. 5. Religion and international
    affairs. I. Blewett, Jane. II. Barney, Kristen R.
    III. Title. IV. Title: Threshold two thousand

GF80.B37 1999   291.1'7836
                     QBI98-1533

CONTENTS

LIST OF FIGURES AND TABLES

ACKNOWLEDGMENTS

This report has been at least twenty-five years in the making. It would not have been possible without the love, support, and encouragement provided by my wife Carol, by our children, Bill, Kris, and Steve, and my father, Richard, and my mother, Gladys, now deceased.

Also essential has been the intellectual and moral support of my extended family, the members of the Holy Trinity Forum. For fifteen years now, these twenty-five friends have met monthly for an evening of discussion of how their faith influences how they live.

My co-authors, Jane Blewett and Kristen R. Barney, have written key passages and made essential suggestions and criticisms throughout the writing process. Their ideas have given shape, structure, and content to the whole document.

The intellectual contributions of several people have been particularly important. Among them are: Fr. Thomas Berry, Professor Jay W. Forrester, Dr. Sallie McFague, Rabbi Herman Schaalman, Dr. S. Z. Abedin, the Reverend Daniel Wee, Bishop Harold Jansen, Dr. Larry Rasmussen, Dr. Alan M. Rulis, Dr. Martha J. Garrett, Mr. Leo Harris, and the Reverend Frank Lee. Trustees of the MILLENNIUM INSTITUTE have also been very helpful in many ways: Mr. Peter H. Aykroyd, Dr. Katharine C. Esty, Dr. Daniel A. Gómez-Ibáñez, Mr. Ronald E. Léger, Dr. Colette Mahoney, Mr. Alan Pilkington, Dr. D. Jane Pratt, Dr. Carlos A. Quesada-Mateo, and Ms. Michaela L. Walsh.

Many others have contributed. The first are those who heard lectures on this material since 1980 and commented on the substance and presentation. A very early draft of the book was presented at a conference sponsored by the Council for a Parliament of the World's Religions at De Paul University, Chicago, on October 13, 1990. The following persons presented helpful comments at that time: Dr. Diane Sherwood, Dr. Aminah B. McCloud, Mr. James Buchanan, Dr. Dennis McCann, and Reverend George F. Cairns. A few months later, the Council for a Parliament of the World's Religions established a committee on critical issues consisting of Professor Ronald Engel, Dr. Daniel Gómez-Ibáñez, Mr. Jim Kenney, Dr. Lois Livezey, Fr. John Pawlikowski, Dr. David Ramage, and Rabbi Herman Schaalman. This committee reviewed the early drafts. Rabbi Schaalman, Dr. Engel, and Professor Livezey made especially helpful suggestions concerning the questions for spiritual leaders that appear near the end of the report.

An oral version of the report was presented November 18, 1992 at the Harvard Seminar on Environmental Values, organized by Dr. Timothy C. Weiskel. Fifteen faculty members and guests from The Divinity School and other parts of Harvard University heard the presentation and many made suggestions for improvements.

The following persons reviewed drafts of the manuscript: Dr. David Peterson, Ms. Laura Peterson, Professor Gordon D. Kaufman, Dr. Daniel A. Gómez-Ibáñez, Mr. Patrick O'Brien, Dr. Glenn Kuswa, Ms. Martha Campbell, Professor Steven C. Rockefeller, Dr. Vivienne Simon, Dr. Robert Goodland, Dr. Herman Daly, Reverend William E. Gibson, Mr. Allan F. Matthews, Mr. Jim Kenney, Dr. Gordon Brown, Ms. Barbara Bernstein, Ms. Diane Brenneman, and Mr. Kip Cooper. Several people have assisted in the preparation and design of the manuscript. Ms. Kristen R. Barney contributed greatly to the design of the figures and prepared most of them; she also designed the format for the report. Mr. Gary T. Gardner also contributed to the work on the figures and to the editing. Ms. Leigh Ann Evanson and Ms. Kirsti A. Lattu typed many of the drafts and helped format the final document. Thanks also to Shirley N. Nunh for proof reading and to Lou Niznik and Craig Gotschall for graphics and photography assistance. Cover design and page layout are by Hare Strigenz Design, Milwaukee, WI, U.S.A.

We are especially grateful to an anonymous donor, Mr. Dan Aykroyd, Dr. Cynthia Harris, Mr. Leo Harris, Mr. John A. Harris IV, Los Trigos Fund, the Mitchell Energy & Development Corporation, the Rockefeller Brothers Fund, the Trinity Grants Program, and the Wallace Genetic Foundation, who have supported the work on this report.

A 1998 edition and printing has been supported by UNICEF-Bangladesh, for which we are all very grateful.

For this new edition, we gratefully acknowledge permission from the Council for a Parliament of the World's Religions for the use here of *A Call to the Guiding Institutions*, Brother Wayne Teasdale for his essay on Spiritual Values, Steven C. Rockefeller and the Earth Council for the use of the *Earth Charter (Working Draft)*, the Lambeth Conference for the statement *World Faiths and Development*, and a 1994 UNESCO Conference for the declaration *Promoting a Culture of Peace*.

Gerald O. Barney, Jane Blewett, and Kristin R. Barney

FOREWORD

At the threshold of a new century and a new millennium, this remarkable book offers a powerful invitation to reflect deeply on the critical issues facing the world. Contained within its pages is a profoundly sobering and yet surprisingly energizing account of what is sometimes termed the world *problematique:* threats to the global environment; divisions within the human community such as racism, interreligious intolerance and hatred, sexual discrimination and exploitation, and xenophobic nationalism; extremes of affluence and poverty; and the prevalence of violence, oppression, and injustice of all kinds.

Threshold 2000 includes all the analysis of *Global 2000 Revisited*, first published for the 1993 Parliament of the World's Religions in Chicago, plus additional materials. That earlier volume helped to focus the attention of leaders and faithful of the world's religious and spiritual traditions on the entire range of modern critical issues. Even more significantly, it addressed the potentially constructive and creative leadership role that the religions can play, singly and collectively, in dealing with the challenges and opportunities of our extraordinary age.

This theme resonated throughout the 1993 Parliament. As preparations for the next Parliament—to be held in Cape Town, South Africa, December 1–8, 1999—begin to take shape, the question takes on even greater significance. Can religion, can the religions, make a difference? In 1993, the query found expression in countless programs and informal conversations throughout the week, but it was perhaps most powerfully addressed in a Sunday afternoon plenary session entitled, "What Shall We Do?" Dr. Gerald O. Barney offered one of the most evocative presentations heard at the 8-day event. His presentation ended with four questions to the planet's religious and spiritual leaders. The questions, set forth once again in this book, demand careful consideration.

"What are the traditional teachings—and the range of other opinions—within your faith on the following issues:

1. How to meet the legitimate needs of the growing human community without destroying the planet's ability to support the community of all life?

2. The meaning of 'progress' and how it is to be achieved?

3. A proper relationship with those who differ in race, gender, culture, politics, or faith?

In addition to the Council for a Parliament of the World's Religions, there are many other interreligious organizations. Some that have evolved in recent years include the Peace Council, comprised of 16 highly respected spiritual leaders, the United Religions Initiative, which is working out its Charter, the Values Caucus at the United Nations, the International Interfaith Centre in Oxford, and numerous local and regional organizations world-wide. These and the more mature organizations are responding to critical issues as part of their interfaith agenda.

4. The possibility of criticism, correction, and reinterpretation and even rejection of ancient traditional assumptions and 'truth' in light of new understandings of revelation?"

These questions lie at the heart of what may well be the most essential dialogue of our time. That dialogue has only begun. The challenges which shape this book can provide a hopeful framework for inquiry and action at every level—from conversations in congregations to national and even global initiatives undertaken by interreligious organizations and by the religious and spiritual communities themselves.

At the 1993 Parliament, an Assembly of nearly 200 respected and influential persons from the world's religious and spiritual communities gave overwhelming assent to a groundbreaking document, *Towards a Global Ethic: An Initial Declaration,* an effort to discover the great ethical commitments which find expression in every religious tradition. At the 1999 Parliament, the Council for a Parliament of the World's Religions will present a new document, addressed to the world's guiding institutions—religion, government, business, education, and media. *A Call to Our Guiding Institutions* will ask them to reflect on and redefine their roles at the threshold of the next century and the next millennium, in light of the very issues, challenges, and opportunities described in *Threshold 2000.* We are delighted that the first draft of the *Call* appears in these pages. After wide-ranging consultations, the final version will be circulated prior to and during the 1999 Parliament.

Clearly, *Threshold 2000* provides a very appropriate context for consideration of the *Call* and of the other remarkable documents which grace these pages. They all suggest new approaches to encounter, understanding, and cooperation between the guiding institutions, and are stirring examples of the insight and influence that religions can bring to bear at this critical time.

Threshold 2000 points the way to a new dialogue—between religions and between religion and the other guiding institutions—about the future of the Earth and the human community. It offers a clarion call to action and, at the same time, a subtle invitation to new modes of insight and understanding. It is a work of worth and substance appropriately emerging at a moment of transition and transformation.

**Dr. Howard A. Sulkin, Chair, Board of Trustees, and
Jim Kenney, Director, International Interreligious Initiative,
Council for a Parliament of the World's Religions**

INTRODUCTION: What shall We Do?

In preparing this book, we have, in a sense, revisited *The Global 2000 Report to the President*, the report I directed for the United States Government on the economic, demographic, resource, and environmental future. Published in 1980, it sold 1.5 million copies in eight languages. *Global 2000* is now 18 years old, and although most of its trends are still disconcertingly accurate, it needed updating.

In 1993, the Millennium Institute assembled new data on most of the basic trends reported in *Global 2000* and published it for the Parliament of the World's Religions as *Global 2000 Revisited*. While updating the analysis, this new book shifted the focus from a policy-making audience to an audience of leaders and members of religious and spiritual communities. That report, printed as Part One of this 1999 edition, was not a full update on the original; only the U.S. Government can do that job, and we hope they will.

In 1998, a new edition of *Global 2000 Revisited*, titled *Threshold 2000*, was published by UNICEF in Bangladesh where the Millennium Institute has been working with UNICEF and other UN agencies, the World Bank, and the Government of Bangladesh. The essay in the Appendix to Part One by Mr. Rolf Carriere, the UNICEF Representative to Bangladesh, describes the connections between the critical issues in that country. Carriere writes that "the choices described in this book as facing the world in the future are the same ones facing Bangladesh today." The floods that increasingly plague Bangladesh and many other countries serve as a dramatic metaphor for the problems we all face.

The Millennial Threshold

Change, big change is needed not only in Bangladesh but throughout the world. Change is difficult, however. The world seems to be in a state of denial and is not responding adequately to the potential problems and stark choices in our future. Even so, the turn of the millennium on the common solar calendar—the 1999–2001 period and beyond—can be a tool for change.

This threshold is like other era-changing and life-giving events such as births, graduations, puberty, and weddings. It is a time when 6000 million people will go from one era to another. It is a time for looking

> There are many changes we humans need to make, and the year 2000 can be a time to encourage us all to make constructive changes of lasting significance. The Millennium Institute's initiative is especially important for Islam and other religions.
>
> While the millennium has special significance for Christians, the year 2000 has international and global significance for all faiths and peoples. The initiative you are taking makes the observance of 2000 into an enormously positive interreligious opportunity.[2]
>
> *Dr. Abdullah Omar Nasseef,*
> *President of the World Muslim Congress*

back at how we arrived at this time and place, and for looking ahead to where we want to go. The "looking ahead" part is more difficult than the "looking back," but several groups are planning important forward-looking efforts. The Millennium Institute is encouraging cooperation among the groups planning to use the occasion to look forward, constructively.

The article titled "World Plans for the Turn of the Millennium" in the Appendix to Part One describes what the Millennium Institute has done and is doing about this important time in world history; it also summarizes some of the major international efforts to bring about constructive change during the millennial years.

Which Spiritual Values?

But what criteria shall we use in making changes? Which values should guide our behavior in a world that is home to numerous religions, spiritual communities, ideologies, cultures and special interests?

> "... we must now understand that our own well-being can be achieved only through the well-being of the entire natural world about us.
>
> *Thomas Berry,*
> **The Dream of the Earth,**
> *1988*

The Millennium Institute is not alone in calling for a new vision, a new concept of progress—and the revitalization of spiritual values. Many thinkers, books, organizations, and members of the human family share in this dream—what Thomas Berry has called "the Dream of the Earth." In an effort to identify appropriate spiritual values, the second part of this book includes several significant documents and other responses to the challenges highlighted in Part One.

The most substantial chapter in Part Two is the first draft of *A Call to Our Guiding Institutions,* based on the declaration *Toward a Global Ethic.* Promoted by the Council for a Parliament of the World's Religions, Hans Küng, Leonard Swidler, Marcus Braybrooke and many others, the effort to define a global ethic based in the world's religious and spiritual communities is the most significant response to the search for global spiritual values.

As a next step in that process, the *Call* presents challenging principles and questions to religious communities and to other guiding institutions that wield so much power. The document also encourages religious individuals, communities, and affiliated organizations to find new ways to cooperate with government, business, education, and media in addressing the critical issues by means of specific actions.

A short statement on "Spirituality in the Community of Religions," by Brother Wayne Teasdale, draws on the world's religious and contemplative traditions to identify characteristics of the terms "spirituality" and "spiritual values." This statement helps to answer the question, "What does the term `spiritual values' mean in today's global and pluralistic world?"

The Earth Charter is a very significant, international document on sustainable development, environmental conservation, and social well-being. Its drafting process is deliberately reaching out not only to secular scientists and professionals, but also to indigenous, religious, and spiritual advisors. This outreach reflects the Charter Commission's commitment to identifying universal values as well as diverse cultural and religious wisdom.

The statement on World Faiths and Development comes from a conference co-chaired by the President of the World Bank and the Archbishop of the Anglican Communion. It indicates renewed appreciation by the World Bank and other development agencies for spiritual and cultural values, for the input of religious leaders, and how such values can be considered in the policies of an international financial institution.

The UNESCO Conferences on the "Contribution by Religions to the Culture of Peace" and the resulting Declaration by spiritual leaders, scholars, and organizational representatives suggest serious efforts to identify the criteria to help us face the challenges of the new millennium.

In addition to the examples in Part Two and in the Appendix, there are many other wonderful projects and visions at work in the world. Emphases vary, and there are some important differences of belief, interpretation, and value among religions and cultures. Yet we need to find areas of consensus—and, happily, there are some! Discovering that consensus, sharing in the visions, and joining the movements is, for many people, an antidote to the despair they might otherwise feel after comprehending the challenges that threaten humanity and the earth.

A striking characteristic of the visions, documents, and hopeful people is the similarity of their themes: that we—humanity, other species and earth—are interdependent; that we face unprecedented crises; that our values and behavior must change if we are to find the optimum path; that all religious and spiritual communities have indispensable roles to play in this process; that all institutions must re-evaluate their commitments in the light of new knowledge; and, despite similarities and consensus, that the diversity of religious and spiritual traditions must be honored.

The choice is before us: to care for Earth or to participate in the destruction of ourselves and the diversity of life.

We must reinvent industrial-technological civilization, finding new ways to balance self and community, having and being, diversity and unity, short-term and long-term goals, using and nurturing.

The Earth Charter,
Benchmark Draft

Yet declarations, visions, and new organizations cannot by themselves change the world's direction. In fact, many of us seem paralyzed by the enormity of the problem. How can we stop the floods? Because that paralysis is fundamentally spiritual in nature, we and the organizers of the Parliament presented questions and challenges to the spiritual leaders of the world who had gathered there in 1993. Now, as we enter the threshold to a new millennium, we invite a much wider audience to engage these issues and accept the challenge of defining appropriate values and behaviors—for ourselves and for our guiding institutions.

What Shall We Do?

My co-authors and I feel an urgent need for a more substantive dialogue between "secular issue" experts and spiritual leaders of all faith traditions. Many pressing issues require thoughtful, holistic attention, integrating both spiritual perspectives and the secular or scientific perspectives. Such integrated work is difficult because of the need for trust, respect, and understanding on all sides.

In the course of my work for the Millennium Institute, I have had many conversations with political leaders and with ecologists, economists, geographers, modelers, political scientists, and other leaders about the role of spiritual traditions in the future of the earth. I have been disturbed by the hostile attitudes that some professionals have expressed toward religious and spiritual traditions.

For example, an internationally famous, highly influential author on sustainable development told me bluntly: "Religion must die. It is the fundamental cause of virtually all social, economic, and ecological problems and much of the violence in the world."

In another example, an ecologist who has devoted his life to the practical work of preserving specific endangered species was equally vehement in his feelings that religion generally, including mine (Christianity), was a menace to the future of Earth. After I explained the importance of my faith to me in the work I do, he was silent for a moment, and then said with total sincerity, "You have done some very important work, but just think of how much more you could have done if your parents had not exposed you to the pernicious influence of religion!"

In one forum or another, virtually every faith tradition is being criticized today for not having a thoughtful, informed, penetrating analysis of the issues facing Earth and Earth's human community in the 21st century, and for not being engaged.

In Part One of what follows, we explain as clearly as possible what we humans are doing to Earth, the implications for us and our children, and the spiritual origins of our hostility to Earth. In Part Two we present some of the international and multi-faith efforts to address the issues raised in Part One. They illustrate some of the efforts in progress, not any final answers.

We, the people of Earth, need the help and involvement of our spiritual leaders. It is from our faiths and their highest values that we derive our sense of origins, of self, of purpose, of possibility. Spiritual leaders can help to transmit these values and the inspiration for what we humans and Earth can become. Hundreds of spiritual leaders addressed the issues of this book at the 1993 Parliament of the World's Religions and will do so again in greater depth at the 1999 Parliament in Cape Town.

Even so, the future choices we face require the active understanding, visions, and participation of all people of good will, not only spiritual leaders, from all communities, whether or not they have religious or spiritual commitments.

We bring this report with our perplexed sense that something is terribly wrong on Earth and with our question: What shall we do?

Along with the growing number of organizations and individuals who are approaching the year 2000 with plans for gifts of service, we believe that this millennial threshold must be the time when six billion of us humans give up our immature, 20th century ways of thinking and living, celebrate our entry into a new era, and then, with renewed purpose and vision, commit ourselves—person by person, family by family, community by community—to the planet-wide effort to create a peaceful, just, and sustainable future.

Gerald O. Barney
President, MILLENNIUM INSTITUTE
Arlington, VA, USA
October 1998

We are all individually and collectively responsible for the common good, including the well-being of future generations.

Declaration on the Role of Religion in the Promotion of a Culture of Peace

PART ONE

Global 2000 Revisited

OVERVIEW

If present beliefs and policies continue, the world in the 21st century will be more crowded, more polluted, less stable economically and ecologically, and more vulnerable to violent disruption than the world we live in now. Serious stresses involving inter-religious relations, the economy, population, resources, environment, and security loom ahead. Overall, Earth's people will be poorer in many ways than they are today.

For more than a billion of Earth's desperately poor humans, the outlook for food and other necessities of life will be no better. For many it will be worse. Life for billions will be more precarious in the 21st century than it is now—unless the faith traditions of the world lead the nations and peoples of Earth to act decisively to alter current beliefs and policies.

This, in essence, is the picture which emerges in *Global 2000 Revisited*. This picture is based on projections of probable changes in the world economy, population, resources, and environment. Although these projections are drawn from the most reliable sources available, they do not predict what will occur. Rather, they depict conditions that are likely to develop if there are no changes in beliefs, public policy, and practices. A keener awareness of the prospects for the 21st century, however, may induce significant changes in beliefs, policies, and practices.

Principal Findings

Rapid growth in the world's population cannot continue through the 21st century and will come to an end either by human decision and action or by an uncontrollable increase in deaths.

Over the past 70 years—roughly one lifetime in many countries—the human population grew from 1.8 billion to 5.3 billion. For every person alive 70 years ago, there are now three. Such rapid growth cannot continue for even another generation. Fertility must decline, or mortality will increase.

But for now the growth continues. Currently the world's population is growing faster than ever before. Each year, 90 million people are added to our numbers, the demographic equivalent of another Mexico. Just a lifetime ago, we were adding only 15 million people per year.

If drastic declines in human fertility (or very large increases in mortality) occur over the next five years, it would be possible to stabilize the human population at about 12 billion within a century. Virtually all of the additional growth—more than 6 billion—would occur in the poorest, least industrialized countries of the world, often called the "South." The population in the South would grow to over 10 billion. The population in the industrialized countries of the "North" would remain at about its current size, a little over 1 billion.

For such a rapid drop in human fertility to occur, it will be necessary to change the religious, social, economic, and legal factors that shape couples' decisions on the number of children they have. Safe and effective contraceptive services must be available, but most importantly, religious teachings and social, economic, and legal circumstances must shift to encourage small families. Child labor, for example, must cease to provide an economic benefit to parents.

It will be difficult to provide 11 to 12 billion people with even such basic necessities as food. Of the 14 billion hectares of land on Earth, only 3.3 billion hectares are potentially arable. At current yields, 0.26 hectares per person are needed to feed the human population; thus at current yields, 3.1 billion hectares would be needed to feed 11 to 12 billion. Only 1.5 billion hectares are currently in production. Since in most cases the best lands are already in use for agriculture, and the remaining lands are already used for grazing or some other use, a doubling of the land in agricultural production would be expensive and disruptive.

Doubling the world's agricultural lands would also cause enormous environmental damage. The potentially arable land that is not now in use—especially land in the tropics—is habitat for a large number of species. Doubling the amount of land in agricultural production would lead to massive extinctions. Even with modest growth in the amount of land in production, a third of all the species that were alive a lifetime ago will become extinct—gone forever—within another decade or two. By 2015, hundreds of species are projected to disappear *daily*.

If we are to meet the food needs of up to 12 billion people by the end of the 21st century, it is essential that agricultural yields continue to be increased—and in ways that are sustainable. Although conventional technologies can probably double yields, there are increasing questions about the sustainability of conventional agricultural technologies. Furthermore, the promised benefits of yield increases through genetic engineering may be delayed and more modest than expected.

The so-called Green Revolution began about 1950. For the first time, yield-increasing technologies (plant breeding genetics, fertilizers, pesticides, and pumped irrigation) were applied extensively and systematically during the last half of this century, increasing yields dramatically and preventing serious food shortages.

But the Green Revolution also changed agriculture radically, making it dependent both on environmentally destructive practices (especially the use of pesticides, fertilizers, and irrigation) and on fossil fuels. Energy used for corn production in the United States, for example, has increased by a factor of four since 1945. The future of human food supplies is now closely linked to the future of energy supplies.

Global energy supplies and prices are likely to become more unstable and erratic in the decades ahead. Even at present rates of consumption, most of the world's petroleum would be burned within the lifetime of a child born today. If consumption were to increase enough to fuel economic growth in the South, the petroleum supplies of the world would disappear even more quickly. The most pressing constraint on the use of petroleum, however, may not be supply of the resource, but disposal space for its principal combustion product—carbon dioxide.

The concentration of carbon dioxide in Earth's atmosphere is increasing around the world, largely because of the combustion of fossil fuels in the industrialized North. Within the lifetime of today's children, global concentrations of carbon dioxide are likely to reach twice pre-industrial concentrations. Such high concentrations are expected to cause planet-wide changes in temperature and weather patterns. Such changes would seriously disrupt agriculture throughout the world as early as the first half of the 21st century, and during the second half would lead to a sea level rise of 20 to 30 centimeters—enough to force the resettlement of hundreds of millions of people and the abandonment of some island nations.

The Choice Ahead

The critical issues described above are just a few of the challenges that lie ahead. Others that have not even been touched on include the implications of AIDS and tuberculosis; nuclear, chemical, and biological weapons; the global debt; migration; corruption; drug trade; and technological change, to name a few.

Given the magnitude of the issues we face, we must expect that within the lifetime of a child born today, the world will change radically in one of two directions. If we continue with present beliefs, institutions, and policies, the world will become highly polarized, with a billion people in the wealthy industrialized countries of the North attempting to enjoy life and leisure a few decades longer while 10 billion plus people in the South spiral downward into increasingly desperate poverty exacerbated by global environmental deterioration. Ultimately the North spirals downward too, and the whole planet drifts off into a new dark age or worse.

But there is another option open to us, one in which everyone comes to recognize that a healthy Earth is an essential prerequisite for a healthy human population. Under this option, the world could become less polluted, less crowded, more stable ecologically, economically and politically if we humans would be willing to work together to: (a) create the religious, social, and economic conditions necessary to stop the growth of human population; (b) reduce the use of resources (sources) and disposal capacity (sinks) by the wealthiest; (c) ensure civil order, education, and health services for people everywhere; (d) preserve soils and species everywhere; (e) double agricultural yields while reducing both agricultural dependence on energy and agricultural damage to the environment; (f) convert from carbon dioxide-emitting energy sources to renewable, non-polluting energy sources that are affordable even to the poor; (g) cut sharply the emissions of other greenhouse gases; (h) stop immediately the emissions of the chemicals destroying the ozone layer; and (i) bring equity between nations and peoples of the North and South.

We do not have generations or even decades to choose between these two directions because of the momentum inherent in population growth, capital investments, technological choices, and environmental changes. In fact, the choice of direction for Earth is being made today.

The choice is difficult because: (a) there is some scientific and economic uncertainty about the severity of the difficulties ahead; (b) it is difficult to believe that such major, unprecedented change can be occurring; (c) it is generally thought to be easier to adapt to whatever comes than to make change in advance of necessity; (d) there is widespread lack of awareness of what is happening; and (e) the steps which must be taken are extremely difficult; and (f) we lack a set of common moral values on which to base collective action. Most difficult, however, is to accept that our concept of progress has failed.

Our concept of progress—our model of development—measures every nation by the norm of a so-called "developed" country. Under this concept of progress, each "rational" nation is to progress to the economic and military might of the "developed" countries of the industrialized North. Similarly, the goal of each "rational" person is to progress to the point of being able to live like the wealthiest. This concept of progress has failed. Twelve billion people cannot live like the wealthiest do now. All nations of the world cannot become as wasteful and environmentally destructive as the industrialized North is now. For them to do so would increase the total economic activity of the world by a factor of five to ten, and Earth could not withstand such an assault.

What is our alternative? What other concept of progress—what other model of development—can we pursue? Currently there is no agreed upon answer to these questions. But if we people of Earth are to avoid a massive disaster within the lifetime of our children, our most critical and urgent task is to bring forth a transformed vision of progress, one of sustainable and replicable development.

We are discovering (or rediscovering) that our human economy is part of, and depends on, the "economy" of the whole ecosphere. So any model for a sustainable world must address both our habits of consumption and reproduction and our willingness to live peacefully with one another, with other creatures, and with Earth itself. Our definitions of progress and success must take into account the future well-being of the entire ecosphere, not just the human part of it. Such a changed understanding of progress and success will require a new understanding of humankind as a species, a new approach to the ethics of interspecies relations, and a new vision for the future of Earth.

Questions for Our Spiritual Leaders

The task before us is fundamentally spiritual in nature: to discover who we humans are, how we are to relate to each other and to the whole community of life, and what we are to do, individually and collectively, here on Earth. So we turn with our questions to you, our spiritual leaders.

What are the traditional teachings—and the range of other opinions—within your faith on how to meet the legitimate needs of the growing human community without destroying the ability of Earth to support the community of all life?

- What does your faith tradition teach about how the needs of the poor are to be met as human numbers continue to grow? What does your faith teach about the causes of poverty? What trends and prospects do you see for the poor?

- How are the needs and wants of humans to be weighed relative to the survival of other forms of life? What trends and prospects do you see for other forms of life?

What are the traditional teachings—and the range of other opinions—within your faith on the meaning of "progress" and how it is to be achieved?

- What does your faith tradition teach about the human destiny? Is the human destiny separable from that of Earth?

- What is your destiny, the destiny of the followers of your faith tradition? What does your tradition teach concerning the destiny of followers of other traditions?

- How are we to measure "progress?" Can there be progress for the human community without progress for the whole community of life?

- How is personal "success" related to "progress" for the whole?

What are the traditional teachings—and the range of other opinions—within your faith tradition concerning a proper relationship with those who differ in race or gender (conditions one cannot change), or culture, politics, or faith?

- Much hatred and violence is carried out in the name of religion. What teachings of your faith tradition have been used—correctly or not—in an attempt to justify such practices?

- Discrimination and even violence by men toward women is often justified in the name of religion. Which, if any, of the teachings of your faith have been used—correctly or incorrectly—in this way?

- How does your faith tradition characterize the teachings and followers of other faiths? Do some adherents of your tradition hold that the teachings and followers of other faiths are evil, dangerous, misguided? Is there any possibility that your faith tradition can derive wisdom, truth, or insight from the teachings of another faith?

What are the traditional teachings—and the range of other opinions—within your faith on the possibility of criticism, correction, reinterpretation, and even rejection of ancient traditional assumptions and "truth" in light of new understandings or revelations?

- Does your faith tradition envision new revelation, new understanding, new interpretation, new wisdom, and new truth concerning human activity affecting the future of Earth?

THE CRITICAL ISSUES

When the United Nations launched the first Development Decade in the 1960s, there was high hope that the nations of the world would move forward in joint efforts to create international systems and structures that would address the urgent needs of the emerging nations of Asia, Africa, and Latin America while assuming the continued growth of the market-oriented industrialized economies. Development would mean more and better for everyone. Progress would guarantee a flourishing economy and technological advancements for the entire world.

Now, four Development Decades later, there is little evidence that the numerous development plans and strategies embraced over the years have done anything to improve significantly the situation of the poor of the world or to enhance the prospects for the wider community of life on Earth. On the contrary, as we look around us today, the struggle for life seems all the more perilous.

Over the whole Earth, the human community and much of the entire community of life is now in serious danger. Problems abound: poverty and starvation, consumerism and population growth, debt burdens and trade imbalances, crime, AIDS, drugs, war and refugees. Most ominously, all of the biogeochemical systems essential for life on Earth, the habitats essential for the survival of diverse species, and even the atmosphere and the oceans are now disturbed and threatened on a planetary scale.

As we humans have begun to think globally, it has become clear that we do not have just a poverty problem, or a hunger problem, or a habitat problem, or an energy problem, or a trade problem, or a population problem, or an atmospheric problem, or a waste problem, or a resource problem. On a planetary scale, these problems are all interconnected. What we really have is a poverty-hunger-habitat-energy-trade-popula-tion-atmospheric- waste-resource problem. This mega problem is so new that we did not even have a name for it until 1970 when the late Dr. Aurelio Peccei described it and named it the "global problematique."

Although Earth is one biologically and environmentally, it is not one socially and economically. Differences between the circumstances of the people in the "North" and "South" complicate discussions of the global problematique.*

Approximately a fifth of the world's people live in the North—the rich, industrialized countries of Canada and the United States, Western Europe, Japan, Australia, and New Zealand. In the North, the per capita consumption of energy and other resources and the per capita generation of wastes (especially carbon dioxide and the various air pollutants that cause acid rain) are extremely high relative to those in the South.

About four-fifths of the world's population lives in the South—the emerging countries of Africa, Asia, and Latin America. In the South there is still rapid population growth, and the environmental impacts (especially deforestation, overgrazing, water pollution and toxic wastes) are largely due to poverty, inadequate education, and inadequately regulated industry.

A clear sense of our future—Earth's future—requires that we examine trends over an extended period. The following discussion will consider developments covering the period 1600 to 2200. While this six hundred year period is only a brief moment in the overall history of Earth, it spans the period during which human activity has had and will have the greatest impact on Earth and is sufficient to provide a context for a discussion of the critical issues of the 21st century. A few events and discoveries that have already occurred during this period are noted in Figure 1.

In thinking about the future it is also important to keep in mind how far into the future our major institutions think. Governments work on a time horizon related to the tenure of elected officials, which is typically less

---

* The terms "developed countries" and "less developed countries" or "underdeveloped countries" are used in economic development literature more or less synonymously with the terms "North" and "South." However, implicit in the terms "developed" and "developing" is the assumption that "developed" countries look like countries such as Germany, Japan, and the United States, and that through "development" all of the world can and should be made to look like "developed" countries. Since the sustainability of the western development model is being questioned increasingly, words are needed which facilitate rethinking the goals of "development" for all nations, including the so-called "developed" countries. The terms "North" and "South," while themselves having many limitations, do not perpetuate an assumption that the western model is the obvious choice for the future.

In addition to the North and the South there is what might be called the new "East"—the countries and republics of Eastern Europe and the former Soviet Union. The Coordinator of the 21st Century Study for the Czech and Slovak Republics, Dr. Pavel Nováček, has remarked: "Are we in Eastern Europe part of the North? I don't think so. We would certainly enjoy the lifestyle of the North, but I think we are too late for that. Are we part of the South? I hope not. We are confused. Our society has collapsed, and we no longer have a coherent national identity or a clear sense of our future."[3]

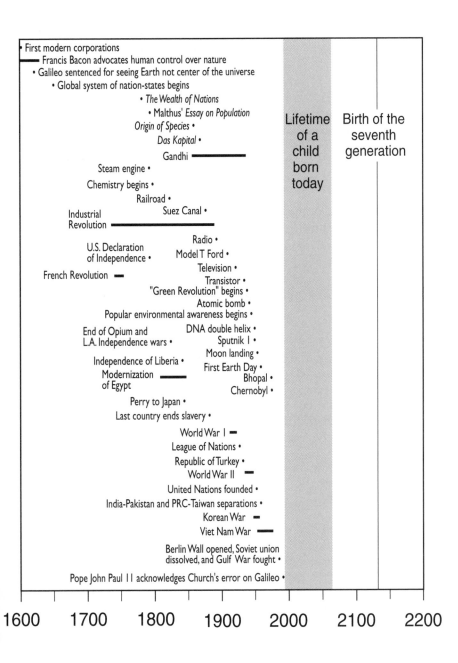

Figure 1: Philosophical ideas, historic events, and scientific discoveries during the period 1600 to present. All figures: Copyright © 1993 by the Millennium Institute. All rights reserved.

than a decade. Market economic decisions typically look ahead about a decade, depending on interest rates. Only the faith traditions of the world have an outlook of generations. Some faith traditions teach that all decisions should be made from the standpoint of their impact on the seventh generation into the future.

To help establish a generational perspective, the shaded columns in all figures in this book mark the seventy-year period that a child born today might live. The line at the right of Figure 1 marks the time of birth of the seventh future generation.

Our Numbers and Basic Needs

When thinking about the future and human needs in the future, it is necessary to consider the number of humans whose needs must be met. To make projections of human numbers in the future, it is necessary to make assumptions about future trends in human fertility and mortality rates. The simplest such assumption—and one that is highly unlikely—is that human fertility and mortality rates in the future will remain just as they are now.

The past history of human numbers and the numbers that the United Nations projects would exist if today's fertility and mortality continued unchanged is illustrated in Figure 2. During the lifetime of adults today, human numbers approximately doubled from about 2.5 billion (1 billion = 1,000 million) to about 5 billion. The time that a child born today might live is illustrated by the gray vertical bar. Much more growth in human numbers can be expected within the lifetime of an infant born today.

A key aspect of caring for the children of the future is food. Since the bulk of our food—98 percent—comes from the land, caring for people for the future requires that we think carefully about land resources and their use.[4]

The total land area of Earth is about 15,000 million hectares (37,000 million acres), but only a relatively small part (about 22 percent) is potentially arable (see Table 1). Most of the land (78 percent) is too wet, too poor, too cold, too dry, or too steep for cultivation. The potentially arable land, which totals about 3.3 billion hectares (8.2 billion acres) is of mixed quality, ranging from highly productive to slightly productive.

Several important aspects of the human dependency on land are illustrated in Figure 3. The straight line across the figure marks the estimated maximum potentially arable land. Approximately half of this total (1.4 billion hectares) is already used for crop production, and much of the remaining less-productive land is already grazed by livestock. Adding to the world's base of arable land or intensifying its use is costly, and additions have slowed dramatically over the last several decades. Consequently, land under continuous cultivation will probably never reach even 3.3 billion hectares.

Equally important, arable land is being lost through erosion, deforestation, expanding urban areas, depletion of irrigation water, salinization, water-logging, and other factors. The effects of these factors on available arable land are illustrated schematically by the downward sloping curve.

The amount of land needed to feed the world population is shown by the curve rising toward the maximum available land. This curve is simply

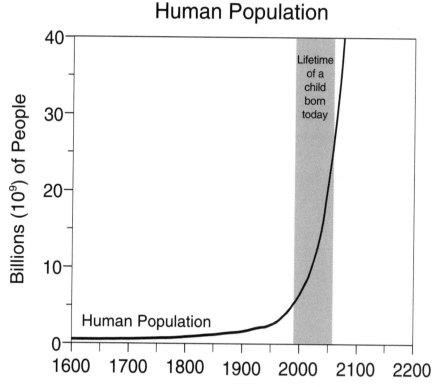

Figure 2: History and projection of the number of human beings whose needs must be met, assuming current fertility and mortality rates remain unchanged indefinitely into the future. Sources: United Nations. 1992. Long-Range World Population Projections: Two Centuries of Population Growth, 1950-2150. New York: United Nations. p. 28; and McEvedy, C. and Jones, R. 1978. Atlas of World Population History, Middlesex, England: Viking Penguin. pp. 342-51.

the curve of human population growth from Figure 2 multiplied by the average amount of land per capita required to feed people—0.26 hectares per person (0.64 acres per person).[5]

In Figure 3 (and several other figures), the curve of land needed to feed the people crosses the curve of land available. Of course in reality it is impossible for this to happen: population cannot increase unless there is food to feed the people. The reason that the two curves cross in Figure 3 and some other figures is that the two curves are projected independently. In reality, as these two curves approach each other, there is a great increase of hunger, starvation, misery, and mass migration, and environmental destruction. Increases in deaths keep the curves from ever actually crossing.

Even now we see examples on our television screens of local areas where the need for land has approached the land available. Local food prices rise and, of course, the poor suffer first and most. The first to die are infants and the old. Before actual starvation (calorie deficiency) occurs, protein deficiency limits children's growth and mental development.[6] A child born today will live to see many people's need for land become much more desperate than today.

Three options are open to us in keeping these curves apart: stopping population growth, preserving arable land, and increasing agricultural

Table 1: *Types of Land on Earth*

Land Types	Area (millions of ha.)	Percent of Total
Highly productive	447	3
Somewhat productive	894	6
Slightly productive	1,937	13
Subtotal	**3,278**	**22**
Too cold	3,725	25
Too dry or steep	5,215	35
Too wet or poor	2,682	18
Subtotal	**11,622**	**78**
Total land area	**14,900**	**100**

Source: U.N. Food and Agriculture Organization. 1989. FAO Production Yearbook tapes. Rome: U.N. Food and Agriculture Organization.

yields. It is sometimes suggested that changing the diet of people living
in the North is a fourth option, but it is not.

The Northern (especially American and Canadian) diet contains a high
percentage of meat. Much of the meat is produced by feeding grain to
animals. The meat produced in this way contains only about 10 percent
of the calories contained in the grain fed to the animals. The idea is that
if Northerners ate lower on the food chain (less meat and more grains
and vegetables), there would be enough grain left over to feed the
whole human population. A change of the Northern diet would indeed
help by shifting the curve over about 15 years (see Figure 4) and would
also, incidentally, improve the health of Northerners. However, a
change of Northern diet cannot by itself solve the problem facing us all.

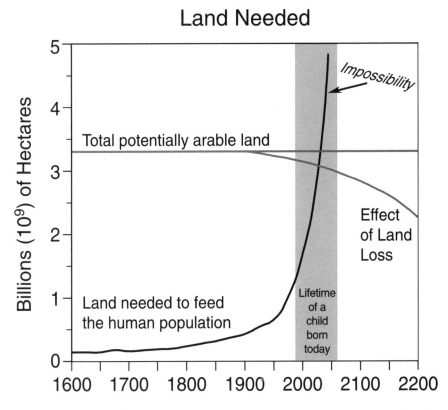

Figure 3: Agricultural land needed at current yields to feed the human population, historical and
projected, and the total amount of potentially arable land. One ha. is equal to 2.47 acres. At current
yields, 0.26 ha. (about 0.64 acres) is needed, on average, to feed a person.

It should also be noted that if incomes in the South were to increase to the point that Southerners begin eating like Northerners (which seems to be the trend among affluent Southerners), there would be a large jump in the demand for agricultural produce (see Figure 4). Such a jump would accelerate the growth in the need for arable land.

For population to stop growing, the number of births and deaths must become equal. This can happen—and has happened historically—either with both births and deaths at a high level or with both births and deaths at a low level. If the deaths are to be kept low and people have long lives, the norm for a person must become one child—two per couple. If this norm were met, the human population would ultimately stabilize after a delay of about forty years during which today's large numbers of youth pass through the fertile period of their lives.

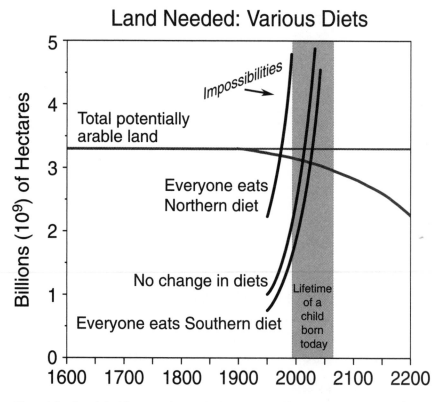

Figure 4: Land needed with current diets, and with hypothetical dietary shifts so that everyone eats either the current Southern diet or the current Northern diet.

The ultimate size of the stable population can be roughly estimated
from what demographers call population profiles. Population profiles
for the countries of the North and South are shown in Figures 5 and 6
for the year 2000. These profiles are, essentially, bar charts. The bars
extend to the right and left of the center for females and males, respec-
tively. Each bar represents the number of people in a five-year age
cohort, for example, the number of males between the ages of 20 and 24.

The profile for the countries of the North is shaped approximately like a
column. This shape is indicative of a stable, non-growing population. It
means that the people in fertile years of their lives (about 15 to 45) are

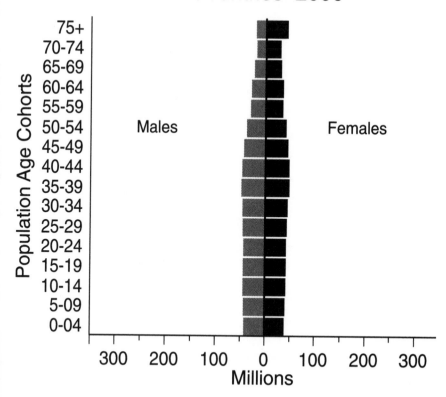

Figure 5: Population profile showing the age-sex distributions for the countries of the North, as
projected by the World Bank for 2000. Source: Bulatao, R. A.; Bos, E.; Stephens, P. W.; and Vu,
M. T. 1990. World Population Projections, 1989-1990 Edition. Baltimore: Johns Hopkins
University Press (for the World Bank). pp. 6-8.

having, on average, about two children, just enough to create new bars at the bottom of the column that are the same width as their own bars. People are just reproducing themselves.

By contrast, the profile for the developing regions is shaped like a pyramid. The pyramidal shape is characteristic of a rapidly growing population. It means that people in the 15 to 45 year cohorts are creating new bars at the bottom that are much wider than their own. The more gradual the slope of the pyramid's sides, the more rapid the population growth.

As population growth slows and stops, the shape of the profile gradually shifts from a pyramid to a column. If somehow by the year 2000

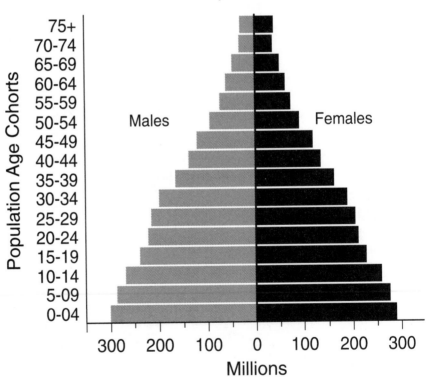

Figure 6: Population profile showing the age-sex distributions for the countries of the South, as projected by the World Bank for 2000. Source Bulatao, R. A.; Bos, E.; Stephens, P. W.; and Vu, M. T. 1990. World Population Projections, 1989-1990 Edition. Baltimore: Johns Hopkins University Press (for the World Bank). pp. 6-8.

replacement fertility (essentially two children per couple) could be achieved throughout the world and if mortality could be kept from increasing, the population pyramid for the countries of the South would ultimately become a column as wide as the base of the pyramid for the year 2000 (see Figure 7). The wide column implies that, barring a huge increase in deaths, the population of the South will grow ultimately to at least twice the number projected for the year 2000. Since in 2000 there will be about 5 billion people living in the South, there might ultimately be 10 billion or more in these countries assuming no increase in mortality rates. In addition there will continue to be a billion people or more living in the North, bringing the world total to at least 11 billion.

The analysis of the previous paragraph provides only a very rough estimate. Recent United Nations projections, prepared with much more

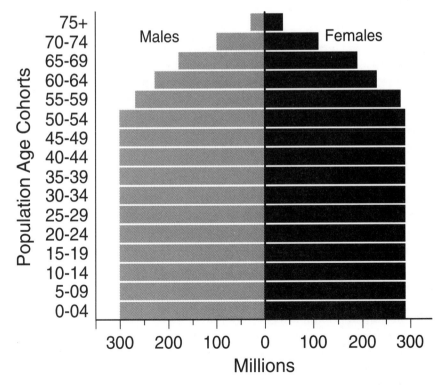

Figure 7: Approximate stable population profile for the countries of the South assuming replacement fertility (an average of 2.1 children per fertile couple) is achieved by 2000.

elaborate methods, suggest that Earth's human population might level off at approximately 12 billion by about 2150.[7]

The magnitude of the change in demographic behavior implied by the U.N. projections can be seen by comparing the historical and projected annual increment to the human population. The annual increment (births less deaths) is an indicator of the additional people for whom housing, jobs, schools, food, etc., are needed each year. As shown in Figure 8, the annual increment to the world population is now rising at a record rate. Approximately 90 million people are now added each year—roughly the equivalent of adding a Mexico every year. According to the U.N. projection, the annual increment will continue to rise to record heights for another few years, peak sharply at about 100 million people per year in 2000, and then fall by roughly three-fourths within the lifetime of today's infants.[8] Should this much-needed event actually come to pass, it would be a truly remarkable change in human reproductive habits, comparable only to the demographic change of the last two decades in China.[9]

Such rapid changes in fertility are extremely difficult to achieve. Currently, large families serve the economic and social interests of couples in most nations of the South. Large families (especially when there are more boys than girls) are perceived as divine blessings and evidence of the virility of the father and the continued fertility of the mother. The children provide free labor, are a source of security in both community disputes and old age, and give status to women and especially to men. Moreover, under current government policies in many countries, children are a relatively low economic burden to the couple. Child labor laws, traditions, religious beliefs, financing of education and health services, the status and education of women, and the norms by which men judge each other's masculinity will all need to change radically if the number of children couples want is to drop to two. There will also need to be increases in the availability of family planning services.

Our Food and the Land

Even if human population is successfully limited to 12 billion, the problem of meeting human needs is not solved. At current yields, over 3 billion hectares of arable land would be required to feed 12 billion people (see Figure 9), and while there are 3.3 billion hectares of potentially arable land available on Earth, the economic and ecological cost of bringing it all into production is prohibitive. An effort to bring 3 billion hectares under cultivation implies an enormous loss of habitat for many entire species and for the critically important wild varieties of human food species. As a consequence, we must also give attention to efforts both to preserve arable land and to increase yields.

The human future is closely linked to the future of soils, and alarmingly little is being done to monitor soil losses and deterioration. Only in the last decade and a half has it been possible to estimate the magnitude and productivity effects of soil loss even in the industrialized countries of the North. Even rudimentary data on soil loss is almost completely unavailable for most countries of the South.[10]

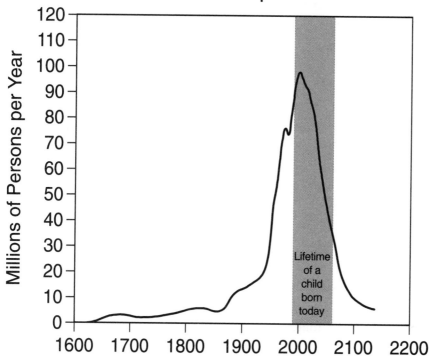

Figure 8: Annual increment to the world's population from 1600 to date and as projected by the United Nations. Sources: United Nations. 1990. World Population Projections. New York: United Nations. p. 21; United Nations. 1992. Long-Range World Population Projections. New York: United Nations. p. 14; and McEvedy, C.; and Jones, R. 1980. Atlas of World Population History. Middlesex, England: Viking Penguin. p. 342.

The arable area currently under cultivation in the world is about 1.4 billion hectares 9,[11] far less than the 3.3 billion hectares potentially arable. Land area under cultivation, however, is increasing only slowly and the rate of increase is declining because the cost of bringing additional land into production is so high.[12] During the 1960s, land under cultivation increased 4.4 percent; in the 1970s, 3.3 percent; during 1980s, less than 2 percent. At the growth rate of the 1980s, arable area might reach about 2 billion hectares by 2200. Should soil losses continue at a mere tenth of one percent (0.1%) per year, land under cultivation would decline almost 20 percent to 1.2 billion hectares by 2200.

Additional perspective on the pressures on arable land comes from trends in per capita arable land (see Figure 10). At the global level,

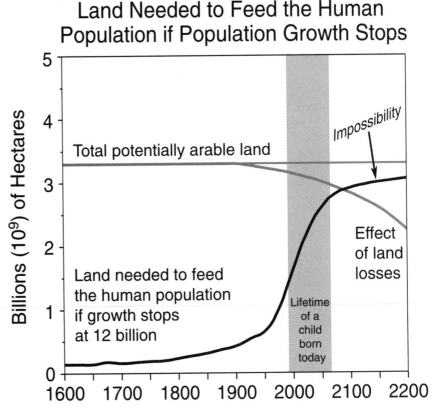

Figure 9: Agricultural land needed at present productivity if population growth stops at 12 billion. Note: One ha. = 2.47 acres. At current yields, 0.26 ha. (about 0.64 acres) is needed, on average, to feed a person.

arable area per capita has declined steadily from roughly half a hectare per capita in the 1950s to less than a third of a hectare in the late 1980s. The countries of the North have experienced a decline from roughly 0.54 hectares in 1960 to 0.47 hectares in 1989. Despite the large increases in arable area in Brazil, Indonesia, and the Sudan, the countries of the South as a group have experienced a severe drop from 0.46 hectares to 0.26 hectares. If one takes into account land losses due to urbanization and other non-agricultural demands, and due to erosion, desertification, waterlogging, and salinization, it is likely that future per capita levels of arable land will drop toward a tenth of a hectare.

Prior to this century almost all the increase in food production was obtained by bringing new land into production, but that is no longer possible. For human numbers to reach 12 billion will involve adding an additional 7 billion, enough to fill the habitable land of every continent

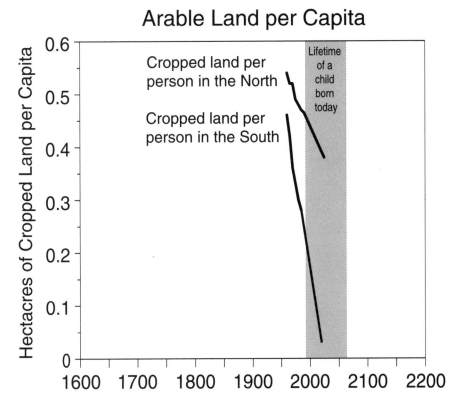

Figure 10: Cropped arable land per capita, actual and projected. The projections are linear extrapo-lations. Source of historical data: U.N. Food and Agriculture Organization. 1989. FAO Production Yearbook tapes. Rome: U.N. Food and Agriculture Organization.

to the density of China and India today. If soil losses and competing uses of land can be stopped completely within a century and intervening losses limited to no more than 15 percent of the total arable land, there might ultimately be about 2.8 billion hectares of potentially arable land, significantly less than the 3.1 billion hectares needed at present yields to feed 12 billion people (see Figure 11). Even with extraordinary efforts to protect and preserve arable land, there is not enough potentially arable land to feed the human population projected for the late 21st century at current agricultural yields. By the first decade of the next century, almost all of the increases in food production must come from increased output per hectare—from higher yields—rather than from increases in arable area under cultivation.[13]

Our Agricultural Yields

The theoretical effects of increasing yields are shown in Figure 11. At current yields about 1.5 billion hectares are needed to feed the human population. If yields were somehow to be doubled, only half as much land (0.75 billion hectares) would be needed, so doubling yields moves each point on the curve down by half.

Similarly, somehow quadrupling yields would move the curve down by three quarters. Note that the effect of the theoretical doubling and quadrupling does not change the shape of the curve but shifts it over and lowers the plateau level. A major human goal must be to find ways to increase yields enough to bring the plateau level below the curve of land available.

The history of yield increases is plotted in Figure 12. Yields increased relatively slowly until modern methods of genetics and plant breeding ushered in the period of the so-called "Green Revolution." The Green Revolution was an enormously significant event in human history.[14] Without it, human needs for land would already have exceeded the land available. As a result of the Green Revolution, yields have increased at about 2.1 percent per year. Furthermore, wheat prices in constant U.S. dollars have declined since the middle of the last century and rice prices have declined since the middle of this century.

While these trends in yields and prices are apparently reassuring, a deeper look raises many concerns about the long- term viability of the trends in input-intensive agriculture.

Mainstream agricultural methods create serious resource and environmental problems: surface and underground water pollution due to run-off of chemicals and animal waste, erosion and compaction of soils, energy dependence (see Figure 13), depletion of underground water deposits, and worker and community health problems. These weaknesses in mainstream agriculture, and alternatives to them are described in two major, path-breaking reports, *Agroecology*[15] and *Alternative Agriculture*.[16]

While these reports provide a critically important service in critiquing mainstream, input-intensive agriculture, they do not provide a sense of agricultural yields to be expected globally in the future. The only recent comprehensive analysis of this extremely important matter seems to have been done by Professor Vernon W. Ruttan, Regents Professor,

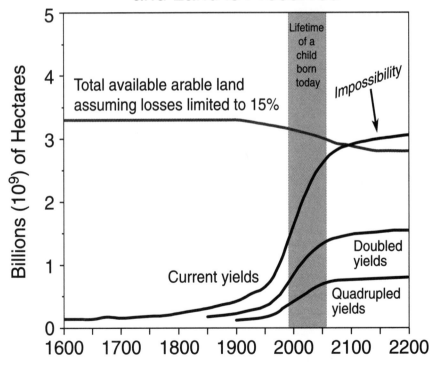

Figure 11: The effects of theoretical increases in yields on the amount of arable land needed to feed the human population: current yields, twice current yields, and four times current yields. Note: One ha. = 2.47 acres. At current yields, 0.26 ha. (about 0.64 acres) is needed, on average, to feed a person.

Department of Agricultural and Applied Economics at the University of Minnesota. The following paragraphs summarize his principal findings:

- For the next quarter century, the primary source of growth in crop production will be applying conventional plant and animal breeding more widely, that is, more intensive and efficient use of water, chemical fertilizers, pest control chemicals, and more effective animal nutrition throughout the world. Although we now have strains of grain that produce 8 to 10 thousand kilograms per hectare under favorable conditions, most of the world's farmers

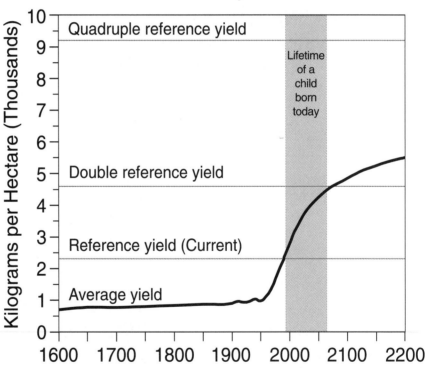

Yield Projections

Figure 12: World agricultural yields from 1600 to present and projections. Sources: For the history: Food and Agriculture Organization, Production Yearbooks; and U.S. Department of Agriculture, Agricultural Statistics. For the projection: Ruttan, V. W. 1990. "Constraints on Sustainable Growth in Agricultural Production: Into the 21st Century." In: Agriculture and Rural Development Department and Training Division, World Bank, eds. 1991. Eleventh Agricultural Symposium: Agricultural Issues in the Nineties. Washington: The World Bank; and Ruttan, V. W. December 1992. Personal communication.

will not achieve such yield gains on their farms without much greater technical knowledge and close working relationships with skilled agricultural researchers.

- By the second decade of the next century, advances through conventional techniques (Mendalian genetics) will be inadequate to sustain the needed yield increases. The incremental response to fertilizer, pesticides, and other inputs is declining. Maximum yield trials in rice have been stuck at 8 to 12 thousand kilograms per hectare for the past fifteen years. Maximum maize (corn) yields are not increasing exponentially but only linearly at about 2 bushels per year. Conventional methods are generally increasing

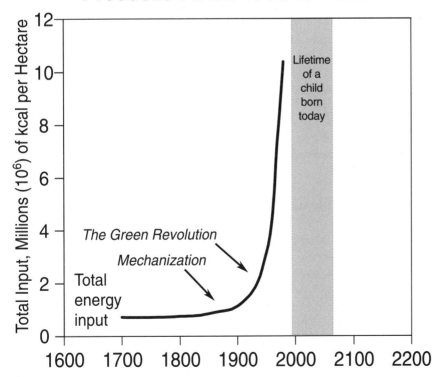

Figure 13: Total energy input to U.S. corn production from 1700 to 1983. Source: Pimentel, D. and Wen, D. Technological Changes in Energy Use in U.S. Agricultural Production. In: Carrol, C. R.; Vandermeer, J. H.; and Rosset, P. M. 1990. Agroecology. New York: McGraw-Hill Publishing Company. p. 152.

only the ratio of grain to roots, stalk and leaves rather than increasing total production of the plant, and since the plant must have *some* roots, stalk and leaves, there are obvious limits to this trend. Conventional animal breeding has produced animals that use a higher proportion of their feed to produce meat and less for general maintenance of the animal, another trend that cannot continue indefinitely.

- Advances in non-conventional methods—microbiology and bio-chemistry—have possibilities for increasing yields later in the next century, but their successful utilization will require major changes in agriculture. Since non- conventional methods are useful only with specific varieties in relatively small geographic areas, research will be needed that is variety and location specific. The research approach will need to shift from "little science" to "big science." Even a small country in the South will need 250 to 300 agricultural scientists if it is to benefit from non- conventional methods. An increasing portion of the products and services will be proprietary or patented and not generally available to countries in the South.

- While one can have reasonable confidence that conventional technologies will continue to increase yields for the next decade or so, conventional technologies are producing a variety of ecological problems and are achieving less incremental gains per unit of research and inputs. In the absence of major changes in agricultural research, it seems likely that the promised gains from biotechnology will continue to recede well into the 21st century.[17]

Our Genetic Resource

All methods of increasing food production are essentially "tinkering" with Earth's ecosystem, and "[t]o save every cog and wheel," wrote the great American naturalist Aldo Leopold, "is the first precaution of intelligent tinkering."[18] We are not saving every cog and wheel. We are throwing away the parts of the ecosystem left and right, as illustrated in Figure 14. By early in the 21st century, species will be vanishing forever at a rate of hundreds per day.

A species that becomes extinct, that disappears forever, can easily be seen as a "nonproblem," since it just vanishes and we hear no more about it. But the rapidly increasing losses of species is a very serious problem. Species are valuable for many reasons.

First and foremost, the *community* of all life is like a sky full of stars, and it is the whole sky full of stars, not human technology, that allows life on Earth to continue. We humans have been making our star to shine brighter and brighter, not even noticing that the other lights in the sky are being eclipsed. Each time we crowd out another species, it is an aesthetic and spiritual loss for all of us. Children born today will have no opportunity to see a third of the species that were here during the lives of their parents and grandparents.

There are pragmatic reasons for concern, too. Both conventional and biotechnical methods of increasing yields require diversity in the germplasm for major crops, but the diversity of available germplasm is declining daily. The wild races and strains of crop plants on which plant

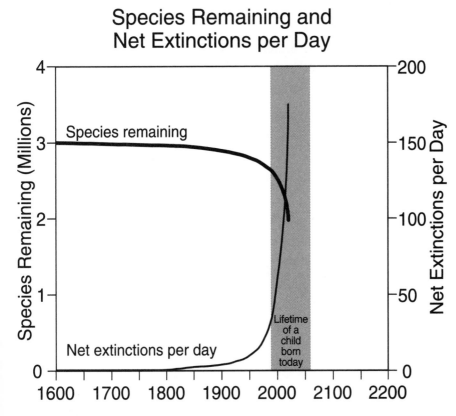

Figure 14: *Species remaining and net extinctions (extinction less speciation) per day, 1600-2020. Source: Raven, P. H. 1987. "We're Killing Our World: The Global Ecosystem in Crisis." Occasional Paper. Chicago: MacArthur Foundation. Raven, P. H. 1993. Personal communication.*

breeders depend will largely be lost over the next few decades as more and more marginal land is brought into cultivation.[19]

Dr. Peter H. Raven, Director of the Missouri Botanical Garden and a world-renowned expert on the diversity of Earth's species, summarizes the practical concerns as follows:

> *In fact, the loss of biological diversity is important to us for many reasons. Only about 150 kinds of food plants are used extensively; only about 5,000 have ever been used. Three species of plants—rice, wheat and corn—supply more than half of all human energy requirements. However, there may be tens of thousands of additional kinds of plants that could provide human food if their properties were fully explored and brought into cultivation. Many of these plants come to us from the tropics.*
>
> *Further, there are numerous uses for tropical plants other than for food. Oral contraceptives for many years were produced from Mexican yams; muscle relaxants used in surgery come from an Amazonian vine tradition- ally used to poison darts; the cure for Hodgkin's disease comes from the rosy periwinkle, a native of Madagascar; and the gene pool of corn has recently been enriched by the discovery, in a small area of the mountains of Mexico, of a wild, perennial relative. Among the undiscovered or poorly known plants are doubtless many possible sources of medicines, oils, waxes, fibers and other useful commodities for our modern industrial society.*
>
> *Furthermore, as genetic engineering expands the possibilities for the trans- fer of genes from one kind of organism to another—indeed, as our scientific techniques become even more sophisticated—we could come to depend even more heavily on biological diversity than we do now.*[20]

One particularly dangerous false and popular notion current today is that with a collection of seeds from endangered species, biologists can restore the ecosystems containing these species, should we ever need them. Scientists cannot recreate lost species, and even if they had all the species, biologists would have no idea, even with billions of dollars and thou- sands of scientists, how to recreate, for example, a tropical rainforest.[21]

Our Energy

The uncertainties about the future of agriculture involve not only future yield increases, but also the fundamental change that modern high- yield methods have brought to agriculture. Agriculture once was a means of capturing solar energy in the form of edible food calories. This is no longer true. Under high-tech, high-yield agriculture, solar energy has essentially become a catalyst for transmuting fossil fuels into food. Food grains produced with modern, high-yield methods now contain between four and ten calories of fossil fuel for every calorie of solar energy. These fossil fuel inputs are for pesticides, fertilizers, tractor fuel, truck fuel, irrigation energy, crop drying, and for other uses (see Table 2). Meat produced by feeding grains to animals contains only about ten percent of the calories contained in the feed grains.

Modern agriculture's dependence on fossil fuels ties the world's food supplies tightly to the world's energy supplies, especially petroleum and natural gas. Already the cost of energy intensive agricultural inputs (fertilizers, etc.) cost farmers 10 to 15 percent of the value of the crop produced.[22]

If agricultural yields are to increase by 100-200 percent, much fossil fuel energy must flow into agriculture. Should energy costs increase, farmers' costs will increase throughout the world, and they will be forced to increase their prices or go out of business. Many people who have become accustomed to eating food grown with energy-intensive, high-yield methods may not be able to afford such food in the future.

While increased yields are important, the ability to grow more food on experimental plots is not enough. A solution to the hunger problem (and the farm problem) requires sustainable methods to grow more food that farmers can sell profitably at prices so low that the neediest can afford to buy it. Since the future of farmers' costs and the future of the world's food supplies and costs are now directly linked to the future of the world's fossil fuels, we must turn to the matter of the future of energy for the world.

There are several sources of commercial energy in use in the human economy today. They include coal, natural gas, petroleum, nuclear fuels (uranium and plutonium), and renewable energy supplies such as fuel wood, water, wind, and solar energy. Electricity is not a source of commercial energy but rather an energy form derived from one of the sources listed above.

For the modern industrial economy, petroleum (oil) has been particularly important because it can be refined into useful fluid fuels (especially gasoline, fuel oil, and kerosene) that have a high energy content per unit of weight and are relatively safe to store, transport, and utilize. In fact, the whole industrial economy of the world is designed primarily around oil-

Then let man look at his Food, (and how Allah provides it): For that Allah pours forth water in abundance, and Allah splits the earth in fragments, and produces therein grain, and Grapes and the fresh vegetation, and Olives and dates, and enclosed Gardens, dense with lofty trees, and fruits and Fodder— a provision for you and your cattle.

The Holy Qur'an 80:24-32

based commercial energy. The future of oil is therefore very important both to development prospects generally and for food production in particular.

Much is known about the future availability of oil. Petroleum geologists have determined by four independent methods that the total amount of oil in Earth when we first started using it in 1900 was about 2,000 billion barrels.[23] This total includes all of the oil known in 1900, all that has been discovered to date, and reliable, stable estimates of all of the additional oil that will be discovered in the future.* In other words, 2,000 billion barrels is all we ever had or will have.

Table 2: *The Energy Input for Various Items Used in U.S. Corn Production*

Item	Energy Input (1000 kcal/ha.))	Percent of Total
Machinery	1,018	9.66
Draft animals	0	0.00
Fuel		
Gasoline	400	3.80
Diesel	855	8.11
Manure	0	0.00
Fertilizers		
Nitrogen	3,192	30.29
Phosphorous	473	4.49
Potassium	240	2.28
Lime	134	1.27
Seeds	520	4.93
Insecticides	200	1.90
Herbicides	400	3.80
Irrigation	2,250	21.35
Drying	660	6.26
Electricity	100	0.95
Transport	89	0.84
Electricity	100	0.95
Transport	89	0.84
Total	**10,537**	**100.00**

Source: Pimentel, D. and Wen, D. Technological Changes in Energy Use in U.S. Agricultural Production. In: Carrol, C. R.; Vandermeer, J. H.; and Rosset, P. M. 1990. Agroecology. New York: McGraw-Hill Publishing Company. p. 152. Data are for 1983, the latest reported.

The outer boundary of Figure 15A represents this initial resource in "Earth's fuel tank." The width of the various compartments in the fuel tank indicate the initial resource—known and yet-to-be-discovered—in North America, South America, the republics of the former Soviet Union, Africa, Europe, Asia-Oceania, and the Middle East.

Since 1900, oil has been steadily drawn from Earth's fuel tank, and this production has lowered the overall level in the tank and altered the relative level in the regional compartments. If current rates of production were to continue unchanged until 2010, the relative levels in the regional compartments would be as shown in Figure 15B. (If the rates of production were to increase to assist in the economic development of the countries of the South, the levels would be still lower.) The shaded area in Figure 15B represents oil remaining; the white area represents the now-empty part of Earth's fuel tank. The regional distribution of oil shown in Figure 15B has significant implications for the world energy market. By 2010, approximately half of the oil remaining will be in a single compartment, the one in the Middle East. As long as several producing regions control more than half of the total resource, the international market can be expected to respond effectively to occasional disruptions in production. By 2010, however, any dislocations in the Middle East must be expected to have global consequences that will be beyond the control of other producing regions.[24]

How long will the fuel in Earth's oil tank last? It is possible to give a reasonably precise answer to this question based on what we know about petroleum and its use. Petroleum production began at zero in 1900 (when petroleum was first produced commercially), and increased at about 7 percent per year through 1973 (see Figure 16). Although sudden price increases in 1973 and 1979 broke the exponential trend in petroleum production, some increase in production is still expected over the next few decades.[25]

Ultimately, however, petroleum production must peak and return to zero when all of Earth's total supply of 2000 billion barrels has been used. By

---

* Oil shale, tar sands, and coal liquefaction might contribute to the fluid fuel resource supply. However, oil shale and tar sands are not competitive at current petroleum prices, and may never be because production of oil from oil shale and tar sands is itself highly energy intensive, and every time petroleum prices rise, the break-even price for production from oil shale and tar sands increases too. Oil shale, tar sands, and coal liquefaction all produce much more carbon dioxide than does petroleum.

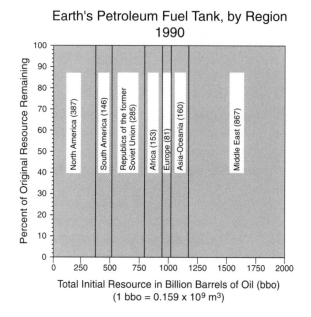

Figure 15A: Distribution of Earth's original (1900) total petroleum resource.

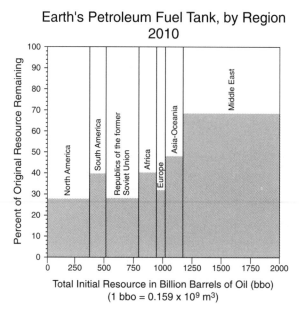

Figure 15B: Distribution of Earth's petroleum resources remaining by 2010, assuming no increase in current rates of utilization. Source: Masters, C. D.; Root, D. H.; and Attanasi, E. D. 1991. "Resource Constraints in Petroleum Production Potential." Science. vol. 253. 12 July 1991. pp. 146-152.

about 2025 a rapid decline in petroleum use must begin. Within the life-time of a child born today, virtually all of Earth's petroleum will be burned, and Earth's fuel tank will have gone from full to empty.

By leveling off oil use at the current rate (about 21 billion barrels per year), it would be possible to delay the fall-off in the availability of oil for perhaps ten or fifteen years, but there will never be large increases in the availability of petroleum to fuel development in the countries of the South. This fact has major implications for the development prospects for both the South and the North.

The industrial style development characteristic of the North is fundamen-tally a process of replacing human labor—man, woman, and child power—with other forms of power derived from commercial energy sources. The energy is needed not only for daily ongoing activities such as powering factories, household conveniences, transportation systems, and energy processing, but also in the construction and maintenance of buildings, roads, equipment, and other economic infrastructure and capital that is now so characteristic of the "developed" countries of the North.

To build industrialized economies modeled on the North, the countries of the South would require enormous quantities of a particular type of energy—fluid fuels. Northern economies are designed to operate on fluid fuels, especially gasoline, because such fuels contain much usable energy for their weight. One gallon of gasoline provides the equivalent of two and a half weeks of human labor.[26] Where could this fluid-fuel energy come from? Not from petroleum, as pointed out above.

The U.S. Department of Energy has investigated probable future prices of petroleum assuming competition from all other sources of energy (see Figure 17).[27] Until the 1973 oil embargo, the average global energy price (in 1982 dollars per barrel equivalent) was approximately $10 and declining slowly. In 1973 the price of oil doubled. Then in 1979, prices doubled again to about $40 per barrel as a result of decisions by the members of the Organization of Petroleum Exporting Countries (OPEC). Since 1979, energy prices have declined as a result of four factors: energy conservation, a slow-ing of the global economy during the early 1980s, increased petroleum pro-duction in the United States and in the North Sea, and the desire of OPEC members for high annual incomes. The outlook now is for prices to increase again toward the end of the century.

These and other petroleum price projections assume only modest increases in the use of energy in the countries of the South. The South is simply not assumed to "develop," meaning that energy use per capita in the South is assumed not to approach that in the North. If instead one assumed substantial development (i.e., substantial growth in per capita energy utilization) in the South, the depletion of the world's petroleum resource would proceed more rapidly and the price increases for petroleum and other forms of energy by the end of the decade would be higher than shown in Figure 17.

The depletion of the global petroleum resource does not present a serious problem if some other form of energy replaces fluid-fuels at comparable prices and without creating serious environmental problems. Although

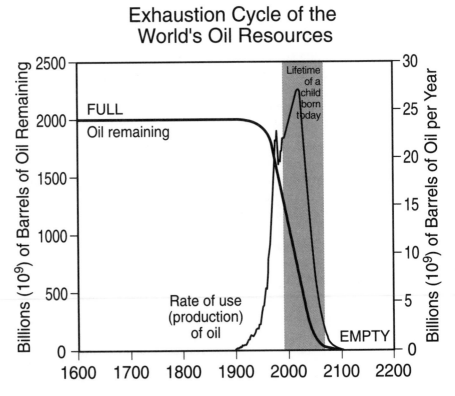

Figure 16: Exhaustion Cycle of the World's Oil Resources. Sources: Masters, C. D.; Root, D. H.; and Attanasi, E. D. 1991. Resource Constraints in Petroleum Production Potential. Science. vol. 253. 12 July 1991. pp. 146-152. DeGolyer and MacNaughton. 1992. Twentieth Century Petroleum Statistics. Dallas: DeGolyer and MacNaughton. p. 4.

there are large coal reserves around the world, burning this coal would produce unacceptable quantities of carbon dioxide, and converting the coal to synthetic fluid fuels (oil or gas) before burning would produce even more carbon dioxide than burning the coal directly. Nuclear,* solar,

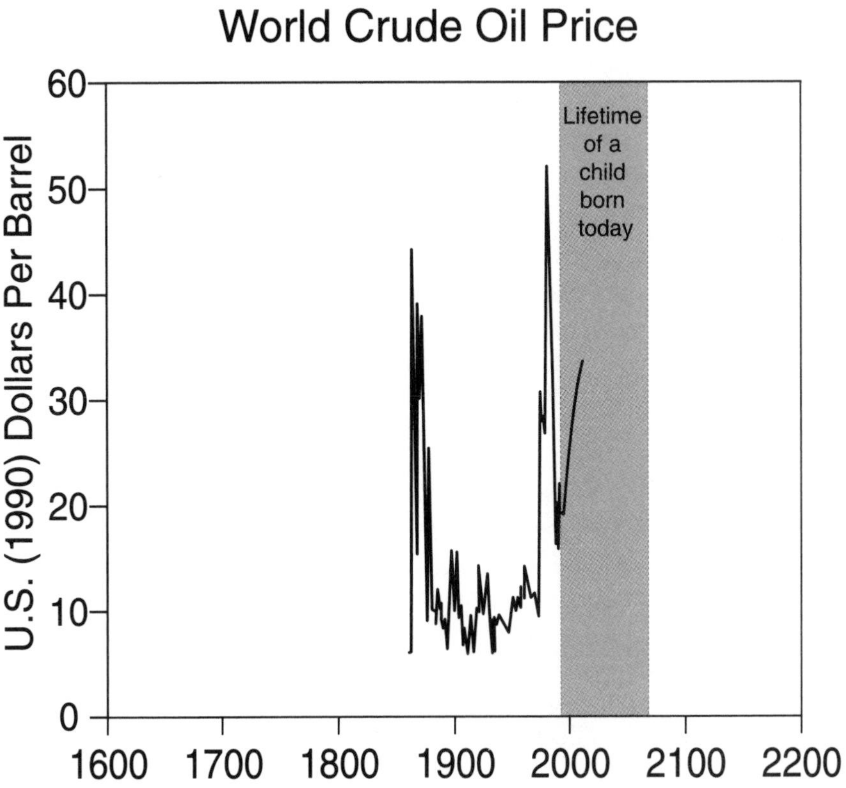

World Crude Oil Price

Figure 17: International price of imported crude oil from 1860 (first commercial oil production) to the present and a mid-level projection, 1990-2010. Source: Energy Information Administration. 1992. Annual Energy Outlook 1992. Washington: U.S. Department of Energy. DOE/EIA-3083 (92). p. 6; and Oak Ridge National Laboratory. 1989. Energy and Technology R&D—What Could Make a Difference? as reported in: U.S. Department of Energy. 1991. National Energy Strategy. Washington: U.S. Government Printing Office.

---

* Nuclear energy also poses unique safety and waste problems. These problems in the Soviet Union contributed to the Soviet decision to end the Cold War. Soviet ex-foreign minister Alexandr Bessmertnykh has said: "[The nuclear reactor accident at Chernobyl] had a tremendous impact. Now we realized the danger of everything nuclear. The accident only had the effect of what one-third of one [hydrogen bomb] explosion would do, and it was devastating."[29]

wind, and thermal power can produce electricity, but cannot produce efficiently the fluid fuels on which all industrial economies now depend. The least costly and least polluting option readily available is to radically increase the efficiency with which energy is used everywhere.[28]

The spectre of the unavailability of energy in a form and quality usable in an expanded global economy has not, as yet, affected the workings of the marketplace. Several decades will be needed to make an orderly transition to a world energy economy beyond the era of petroleum. We are already at the point of needing an alternative to the petroleum economy, and yet no transition is in progress to an energy economy that will meet the needs of all peoples. Yet, as can be seen in Figures 16 and 17, there has been essentially no response by the market mechanism.

Part of the reason for the lack of action on global energy for sustainable development is the United Nations System of National Accounts (UNSNA). Under this system, the primary measure of how well a nation's economy is doing is the Gross Domestic Product (GDP), which is a measure of the total goods and services produced by a country during a year. This grading system for nations takes no account of declining "natural capital" such as oil deposits. In fact, under the UNSNA a nation's resources have "value" only after they are used. The faster a nation converts its resources (for example, petroleum) into "goods" and its "goods" into wastes—the faster the "throughput" of resources to waste and pollution—the higher the nation's marks on the GDP scale. Even the $1 billion cost of the grossly inadequate cleanup after the Valdez oil spill in Alaska increased the U.S. GDP, giving the totally false impression that oil spills are good for the U.S. and other economies.

Although efforts are being made to revise the UNSNA,[30] there is strong resistance to change. Part of the resistance to change is based on a strong faith that the greed and self-interest underlying the market mechanism foresee all economic, resource, and environmental problems, and that the market mechanism will steer the ship of state safely through the rocks ahead. The difficulty is that the market mechanism is so short-sighted that it can scarcely see beyond the bridge and certainly not as far as the rocks ahead.

The limited foresight provided by the market is a result of basing market decisions on "present values." There are three difficulties with this approach. First, the market mechanism works only for those who have the money necessary to be a part of the market. This is why, as far as the market mechanism is concerned, countries of the South are not now and never will be of a significant factor in world petroleum markets.

Second, the present value method of valuing future costs and benefits, which is now incorporated into all business calculators, allows individuals and corporations in a market system to look ahead, only as far as the discount rate (essentially the prevailing interest rate) permits— about ten years at a 7 percent discount rate, seven years at 10 percent, and about one year at 70 percent. The higher the interest rate, the more short-sighted market decisions become. For the market mechanism to look ahead, the decades needed to develop a new global energy system would require interest rates everywhere to be kept in the range of 1 percent to 2 percent.

Some faith traditions say that all societal decisions should be made based on the welfare of the seventh generation in the future, which means considering costs and benefits for the whole society about 140 years into the future. For the market to consider the interests of the seventh generation, interest rates would have to be kept below half of one percent (0.5%).

The third difficulty with present values is that they weigh future costs and benefits *to the individual or corporation making the decision*, and as a result, costs and benefits to the society as a whole are ignored as "externalities." Successful market-oriented national economies have developed many institutions and procedures to limit the neglect of externalities such as pollution and to control false advertising, dangerous products, and abuse of labor. The former centrally-planned economies of the world lack not only the entrepreneurial experience required in a market economy but also the regulatory institutions that limit the most rapacious and destructive aspects of capitalism. It is no wonder that they are finding the transition from a planned economy to a market economy difficult.

The market mechanism, as it functions in international trade, strongly favors the industrialized countries of the North and multinational corporations. The key international agreement concerning international trade is the General Agreement on Trades and Tariffs (GATT). Currently the GATT agreements encourage the sale of Southern resources to the North at unreasonably low prices, encourage practices that bring toxic pollutants to the South, accelerate the destruction of genetic resources in the South, and discourage value-added processing of resources of the South.[31]

The point is simply this: Decisions concerning the global energy economy would be very different if they were based on the costs and benefits to the seventh generation and on a different system of national accounts. The future costs of present resource consumption, waste production, and pollution generation would then not be ignored. As things are, the limited world supplies of petroleum and the inability of the market mechanism to stimulate an early transition to a new global energy economy that can accommodate development in the South mean that the countries of the South face an impossible task of development, at least as "development" is now understood.

Our Environment

Human numbers, wealth, poverty, technology, and beliefs are now having planet-wide consequences.[32] The energy and agricultural scenarios sketched above have several large environmental implications. One of particular concern is certain chemicals that human activities are releasing into the atmosphere. Some of these chemicals are altering the planet's temperature- regulating systems, threatening to change the climate and temperature of the whole Earth. Others are depleting Earth's protective layer of stratospheric ozone, increasing the amount of dangerous ultraviolet light reaching ground level.

The greenhouse gases

A number of so-called "greenhouse gases" have the property of allowing high frequency solar radiation to pass through the atmosphere to the surface of Earth where the radiation is absorbed, providing warmth to Earth. These gases (carbon dioxide, chlorofluorocarbon 12, methane, chlorofluorocarbon 11, nitrous oxide, ozone (stratosphere), ozone (troposphere), and other chlorofluorocarbons) block the transmission of low frequency heat radiation back into space. The net effect of the greenhouse gases is to trap solar energy and keep the temperature of Earth within a range in which approximately 3 million species can live. Increased concentrations of greenhouse gases can disrupt the operation of the planet's temperature-regulating systems and cause the temperature of Earth to rise.[33]

Currently, the concentrations of all greenhouse gases are rising. Most alarming are the growing concentrations of carbon dioxide (see Figure 18). Northern transportation and industry are the principal sources, but Southern deforestation is also very significant.

As a result of the increasing concentrations of the greenhouse gases, the temperature of the entire planet is expected to begin increasing soon. The best estimate currently available of global temperature change comes from the Intergovernmental Panel on Climate Change (IPCC), which has been established jointly by the World Meteorological Organization and the U.N. Environment Programme. The IPCC estimates that the average temperature of the planet will increase by about 2.5°C by 2100 (see Figure 19).[34]

For the first time in 1991 the effect of ozone depletion (discussed below) on the overall temperature of Earth was calculated and measured. It was found that ozone depletion cools Earth so much that ozone depletion may have offset and masked a significant part of the temperature increase to be expected from greenhouse gases over the past decade.[35]

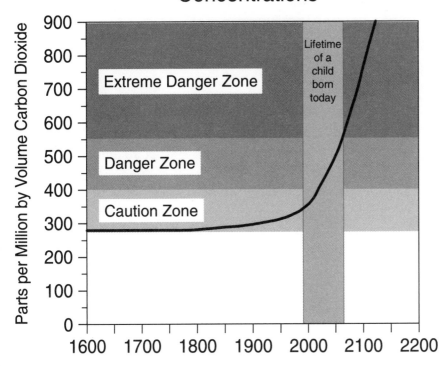

Figure 18: Carbon dioxide concentrations, historical and projected. Source: IPCC Working Group I. June 1990. Policymakers Summary of the Scientific Assessment on Climate Change. "Business-as-usual" scenario. Nairobi: U.N. Environment Programme. pp. 7-9.

On first hearing, an increase of 2.5°C does not sound alarming. Local day-to-day temperature changes are much larger. On a planetary scale, however, an increase of 2.5°C has enormous significance. It is a change of a magnitude unprecedented since the last ice age 10,000 years ago. Furthermore, the pollutants causing this global disaster are expected to continue accumulating in the atmosphere for at least several decades (see Figure 18), so the ultimate temperature rise could easily be even larger.

A major concern associated with temperature increase is a rise in the sea level and the flooding of low-lying coastal areas. Nearly a third of all

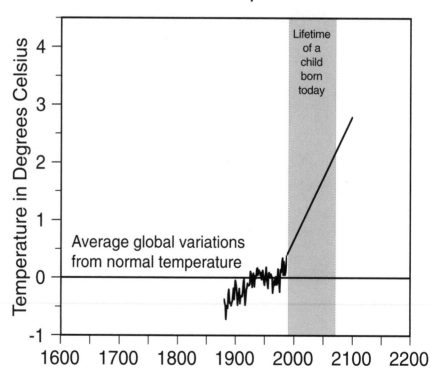

Figure 19: Average global variations from normal temperature, 1880-1988 and projection to 2100. Projections are from Scenario IS92a as presented in Intergovernmental Panel on Climate Change. 1992. 1992 IPCC Supplement. Nairobi: U.N. Environment Programme. p. 25. The historical data are from Hanson, J. E. 1988. As reported in Shabecoff, P. "Global Warming Has Begun, Expert Tells Senate." The New York Times. 24 June 1988. p. A1.

humans live within 60 km (37 miles) of a coastline, and some of the world's most productive biological systems are also in coastal areas. The IPCC projects a sea-level rise of 60 cm by 2100 unless corrective measures are taken very soon. This projection takes into account both thermal expansion of sea water and melting of glaciers. Even if increases in greenhouse gas concentrations were to stop suddenly in 2030, the momentum of change would cause an increase in the sea level of 40 cm by 2100.[36]

The impacts on human settlements and the whole community of life are large. A 20-30 cm sea-level rise poses problems for low-lying coastal zones (for example, much of Bangladesh) and for island countries. Such a rise will destroy productive land and freshwater resources. A 100 cm rise (the high projection for 2100) would destroy several countries, displace large populations, destroy low-lying urban infrastructure, inundate productive lands, contaminate freshwater supplies, and alter coastlines. These effects could not be prevented except at enormous cost.[37]

Other effects of 2.5°C global warming will vary greatly from region to region. Some areas will experience only a modest temperature increase of a degree or so; other areas will experience changes two or more times the average. Major cropping areas of the world will be shifted, causing dislocations and disruptions. Exactly where these shifts will occur is beyond the predictive capabilities of current models on even the largest supercomputers. If cropping areas should move into regions of poorer soils, yields would likely fall or food become more expensive because of the additional fertilizer needed to maintain yields. As cropping areas move, existing agriculture infrastructure, capital equipment, and farm labor will be idled, and in the new areas infrastructure, capital, and labor will be inadequate to take advantage of the new conditions.

With increased carbon dioxide concentrations, crop plants will grow faster, but weeds will grow faster, too. In some areas, especially in sub-Saharan Africa, the growth of weed species is expected to increase more than the growth of crop species.

As air warms, its capacity to hold moisture increases, and this implies changes for Earth's hydrologic cycle. Most climate models project an overall increase in precipitation of 7-11 percent from 1960-2030.[38] Increased evaporation rates, however, would lead to dryer soils in major cropping areas, a situation with adverse implications for seed germination rates and crop yields. Greater fluctuations in river flows will increase the damage done by droughts and floods. The stress on dams, reservoirs, channels, and dikes will also be increased as these important facilities experience more frequent storm flows that exceed their design capacity.

Some cities would become much warmer. Currently temperatures in Washington, DC, for example, exceed 100°F only one day per year and 90°F only 35 days per year. By 2030, there could be 12 days over 100°F and 85 days over 90°F. Other cities around the world can expect similar changes.

The ozone layer

Part of the radiation the sun sends toward Earth is harmful to virtually all forms of life. Fortunately, there is a layer of stratospheric ozone surrounding Earth that absorbs and blocks much of this harmful radiation, which is known as ultraviolet B, or simply UV-B. Without the protection of this invisible ozone shield, all life on Earth would be endangered by UV-B radiation.

In 1985 scientists discovered, quite by accident, a continent-sized "hole" in Earth's ozone shield over Antarctica. (Measurements showing the formation of the hole were actually made by instruments on a satellite in the late 1970s, but the measured concentrations of ozone were so low that they were disregarded for years as an "obvious" measurement error.) The hole varies in size and depth from season to season. In some spots the ozone has been found depleted by as much as 60 percent. Figure 20 shows ozone declines measured in the ozone hole.[39]

The discovery of the "hole" in the ozone layer was a total surprise. No scientific theory and no computer model predicted the possibility of such a hole, and a full scientific explanation has still not been developed. No one knew if the hole would spread, endangering life over the whole planet.

As soon as the extremely low measurements of ozone concentrations were recognized as valid, intense research efforts were begun to determine the cause of stratospheric ozone depletion, to predict future trends, and to assess the ecological consequences of increased UV-B radiation. As a result of this research it is now known that the release of the chemicals shown in Table 3 adversely affect ozone concentrations. Chlorofluorocarbon (CFC) chemicals do 80 percent of the damage to the ozone layer. A decade or more is needed for these chemicals to migrate from the surface of Earth to the stratosphere, and once there, they catalyze ozone-depleting reactions for 75-110 years. Each CFC molecule can destroy 100,000 molecules of ozone. A 1 percent reduction of stratospheric ozone increases UV-B radiation at Earth's surface by 2 percent.

An increase in the amount of ultraviolet radiation will cause an increased number of cancers, especially skin cancers in humans and other animals. Scientists estimated that a 1 percent increase in UV-B would result in a 2 percent increase in skin cancers of light-skinned people.[40] (Dark-skinned people are not as susceptible.) Caught early, wart-like melanoma tumors can be cured by surgical removal, but once the malignancy spreads to other parts of the body, it is among the most lethal and aggressive of cancers, resisting both chemotherapy and radiation treatment.

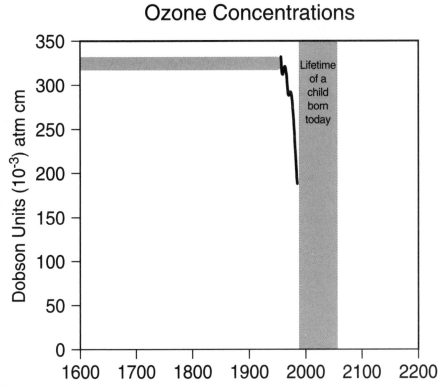

Figure 20: Total ozone concentrations above Halley Bay, Antarctica. Source: Global Environmental Monitoring System. 1987. The Ozone Layer. Nairobi: United Nations Environment Programme. p. 23; and Bowman, K. P. 1988. "Global Trends in Total Ozone." Science. 1 January 1988. pp. 48-50. Watson, R. T. and Albritton, D.C. 1991. Scientific Assessment of Ozone Depletion: 1991. Geneva: World Meteorological Organization, p. ES-v. Note: Although there are no data on ozone concentrations above Halley Bay earlier than 1957, many scientists feel the very constant concentrations during the 1957 to 1970 period probably extend well back in time, as shown in the figure.

In addition to increasing melanomas, more exposure to UV-B radiation increases the general susceptibility to all cancers and infections. This is because exposure to UV-B impairs the effectiveness of the body's immune system, which helps fight cancer cells as well as infections.

An increase in UV-B would also increase the incidence of cataracts and other eye disease. The human retina is especially sensitive to damaging sunburn, but since there are no pain sensors in that part of the eye, we do not feel the burning.

Many crop plants and forest species are adversely affected by ultraviolet light. UV-B can slow growth, interfere with germination, damage plant hormones and chlorophyll, and, as a result, reduce the total plant mass produced during the growing season.

UV-B penetrates several meters in clear water and threatens many aquatic organisms. Single-celled algae, the beginning of the aquatic food chain, are seriously threatened. Experiments show that all anchovy larvae are killed to a depth of 10 meters by 15 days' exposure to UV-B at an intensity 20 percent higher than normal.

In September 1987, representatives of 24 countries met in Montreal to consider the problem. As with the greenhouse gases, the ozone-depleting chemicals are produced primarily by the wealthy, consuming countries

Table 3: *Trace Gases Affecting Ozone Concentrations*

Gas	Average lifetime in atmosphere (years)	Average global concentration (ppbv)	Annual rate of increase (percent)
CFC-11	75	0.23	5
CFC-12	110	0.4	5
CFC-113	90	0.02	7
Halon 1301	110	very low	11
nitrous oxide	150	304	0.25
carbon monoxide	0.4	varitable	0-2
carbon dioxide	7	344,000	0.4
methane	11	1,650	1

Source: UNEP/GEMS. 1987. "The Ozone Layer." Nairobi: United Nations Environment Programme.

of the North. CFCs are used in aerosols, refrigeration equipment, solvents, and foam producing agents, and there was reluctance on the part of Northern industrial and political leaders to ban them entirely. Instead, the Montreal Protocol called for a 50 percent reduction in CFC production in the 24 signatory countries by 1997.

Following the 1987 meeting, evidence accumulated that the protective ozone shield was thinning more rapidly than expected and that less damaging chemicals and processes could be developed more quickly and less expensively than industry leaders had expected. In 1990 the treaty's signatories met in London and adopted a deadline for phasing out the most damaging chemicals by 2000.

In 1992 the signatories (now 87 countries) met again and agreed to move up the phase-out deadlines as follows: 1996 for chlorofluorocarbons, 1994 for halons, and 2030 for hydro-chlorofluorocarbons. For methyl bromide, a previously unregulated ozone-depleting pesticide, it was only agreed to limit 1995 production to 1991 levels.[41]

The situation at present is dangerous but hopeful.[42] From 1979 to 1992, the amount of total column ozone has decreased over most of the planet. Worldwide losses in 1992 were the largest ever recorded, probably due in part to the debris injected into the stratosphere by the 1991 eruption of Mt. Pinatubo in the Philippines. There are now for the first time significant decreases in ozone concentrations during the spring and summer in both the northern and southern hemispheres at the middle and high latitudes, where most humans live.

The ozone hole over Antarctica has become larger and deeper. Ozone losses have also been observed now over the Arctic, but no massive hole comparable to that over the South Pole has opened in the North.

There is strong evidence now that the ozone depletion is due primarily to chlorine and bromine containing industrial chemicals. Since stratospheric abundances of chlorine and bromine will increase at least until 2000, significant further losses of ozone must be expected at middle latitudes and in the polar regions.

Large increases in ultraviolet light have been observed at ground level in Antarctica. In the mid-latitudes, increases of ultraviolet light of about 12 percent occurred during the 1992-93 season of depletion, which now extends into the summer months.

If the Montreal Protocol is strengthened to limit further the emissions of chlorine and bromine-containing compounds, *if* all countries sign the protocol and fully comply with its provisions, and *if* no further surprises develop, the damage done to Earth's protective ozone shield might be repaired within about 100 years. A hundred countries (including India and China), however, have not signed the protocol.

Our Poverty, Violence, Hatred, and Despair

The issues discusses above—population, food, land, energy, species, climate change, stratosphere, ozone depletion—are all interrelated, and many other issues could be added to the list. The unchecked pandemic of the virus that causes AIDS has not even been mentioned. Nor has the reemergence of tuberculosis as a major disease that is furthered by AIDS, homelessness and poverty and that may kill even more people than AIDS. Nor has the global debt problem been mentioned, and the fact that net capital flows are now from that South to the North rather than from the North to the South. Water problems—both quantity and quality—are rapidly developing virtually everywhere. While the Cold War seems to be at an end, nuclear weapons having destructive power equivalent to 5,000 times all the weapons used in World War II are still with us, and the nuclear weapons in the former Soviet Union are now under looser control than earlier. Toxic and radioactive wastes continue to accumulate with no satisfactory disposal methods in sight. Corruption, especially when related to drug trafficking, is bringing tragedy and despair to many communities and countries. The technologies needed to produce biological and chemical weapons, conventional weapons, and terrorist bombs are now much more widely available. Patent laws reward wealthy countries that can afford education and research and penalize poorer countries that can't. Education itself has become vital to the security and prosperity of every country. One could go on and on.

But there is one more issue that stands out from all the rest: What we are doing to Earth, we are doing to ourselves. The breaking of life-sustaining relationships in the biosphere parallels the breaking of life-sustaining relationships in the human community, our most critically important resource.

An old story from the book of Genesis in the Jewish *Torah* provides an illustration:

> *So Abram went up from Egypt, he and his wife, and all that he had and Lot with him, into the Negeb.*

*Now Abram was very rich in cattle, in silver, and in gold... And Lot... also
had flocks and herds and tents, so that the land could not support both of
them dwelling together... and there was strife between the herdsmen of
Abram's cattle and the herdsmen of Lot's cattle...*

*Then Abram said to Lot, "Let there be no strife between you and me, and
between your herdsmen and my herdsmen; for we are kinsmen. Is not the
whole land before you? Separate yourself from me. If you take the left hand,
then I will go to the right; or if you take the right hand, then I will go to
the left. And Lot lifted up his eyes and saw that the Jordan valley was well
watered everywhere like the garden of the Lord... So Lot chose for himself
all the Jordan valley... Abram dwelt in the land of Canaan...* [43]

This is the story of two wealthy families that together could not be
supported by the land. As the environment deteriorated and adversely
impacted their wealth (cattle) and income, there was fighting between
their servants. To preserve family unity, Abram wisely proposed that the
two families part and live separately where the land could support them.

Abram's solution worked again and again for centuries. As long as "the
whole land was before [us]," we could separate, migrate from country to
country, continent to continent and settle where the land could support
us. But the whole land is no longer before us. Now that we are 5 billion,
much of the land cannot "support [us] dwelling together," and there is
no well-watered Jordan valley waiting to be settled.

How will we respond now that the whole land is no longer before us?
How will we respond when the deteriorating environment and resource
base impacts on our wealth and income? Probably we will respond the
same way that Abram's and Lot's herdsmen responded: in strife.
Probably there will be more violence, hatred, and despair.

Already there are conflicts between communities and nations over land,
water, oil, fish, "pollution rights," acid rain, genetic resources, forests,
and many other resources. And such conflicts can be expected to inten-
sify and to exacerbate already frayed relationships between nations,
between women and men, between adults and children, and between
peoples of differing cultures, races, and faiths. Some of the conflict will
be motivated by greed, some by extreme poverty, and some by despair.

In Zaïre , for example, it is greed and corruption. Despite the fact that
Zaïre has rich deposits of cobalt, copper, and diamonds and rich agri-

cultural lands, clean water, and inexpensive electric power, the World Bank in 1992 ranked it as the world's 12th poorest country with income of $220 per capita. The reason is primarily corruption and repression led by President Mobutu Sese Seko himself. Mobutu treats the country's funds as his own and has chateaux in Spain and Belgium and other major properties in Paris, Monte Carlo, Switzerland, Portugal, and the Ivory Coast. The repression is brutal. Soldiers in plain khaki uniforms— the so-called "Owls"—roar through the capital most nights in unmarked vehicles attacking and killing uncounted people considered political threats to Mobutu.

In September 1992 tensions were high after Mobutu canceled a national political conference called to draft a new constitution and schedule a multi-party election. Then a group of Mobutu's elite soldiers, angry because they had not been paid, began looting and burning the city. Soon civilians joined in. In short order, the industry was destroyed and the housing burned. Medical and other professionals fled, followed by foreign nationals and their investments, and everyone else who could leave. In just a week the trust that held the society together vanished and the society with it.[44]

The story of the Ik told by anthropologist Colin Turnbull is another example of how the resource of "community" can vanish. The Ik, a tribe of nomadic hunters in the mountains separating Uganda, Sudan, and Kenya, lost their hunting area and were forced to become "farmers" in an area not suited to settled agriculture. The result was chronic near-starvation for everyone and reduction of life expectancy to perhaps 20 years. Over the course of just three generations, the society lost all of the qualities we normally think of as human. Walled into compounds and fearful of each neighbor, their only goal was individual survival. A man and a woman no longer married for love, but because each thought they knew how to exploit the other. The only remaining concept of "good" was associated with food: A good person was a person with food— nothing more, nothing less.

Turnbull's story of Adupa, one of the Ik children, and her "insane" attempt to preserve love in her family and community illustrates what can happen to human values as environmental conditions and human community deteriorate.

> *Hunger was indeed more severe than I knew, and the children were the next to go. It was all quite impersonal—even to me, in most cases... But Adupa*

was an exception. Her stomach grew more and more distended, and her legs and arms more spindly. [She was mad, and her] madness was such that she did not know just how vicious humans could be...

Even worse, she thought that her parents were loving... Adupa... brought them food that she had scrounged from somewhere. They snatched that quickly enough. But when she came for shelter they drove her out, and when she came because she was hungry they laughed,.... as if she had made them happy...

Partly through her madness, and partly because she was nearly dead anyway, her reactions became slower and slower. When she managed to find food— fruit peels, skins, bits of bone, half-eaten berries, whatever she held it in her hand and looked at it with wonder and delight, savoring its taste before she ate it. Her playmates caught on quickly, and used to watch her wandering around, and even put tidbits in her way, and watched her simple drawn little face wrinkle in a smile as she looked at the food and savored it while it was yet in her hand. Then as she raised her hand to her mouth they set on her with cries of excitement, fun and laughter, beat her savagely over the head and left her.

I took to feeding her, which is probably the cruelest thing I could have done, a gross selfishness on my part to try and salve and save, indeed, my own rapidly disappearing conscience. I had to protect her, physically, as I fed her. But the others would beat her anyway, and Adupa cried, not because of the pain in her body, but because of the pains she felt at that great, vast empty wasteland where love should have been.

It was that that killed her. She demanded that her parents love her. She kept going back to their compound... Finally they took her in, and Adupa was happy and stopped crying. She stopped crying forever, because her parents went away and closed the asak tight behind them, so tight that weak little Adupa could never have moved it if she had tried. But I doubt that she even thought of trying. She waited for them to come back with the food they promised her. When they came back she was still waiting for them. It was a week or ten days later, and her body was already almost too far gone to bury. In an Ik village who would notice the smell? And if she had cried, who would have noticed that? Her parents took what was left of her and threw it out, as one does the riper garbage, a good distance away...[45]

Turnbull observed and wrote about the Ik into the early 1970s, and since then many other communities have experienced the forces of poverty, oppression, violence, and hatred that destroy communities and create despair. In most cases, there was no anthropologist like Turnbull there

If we do these things in the greenwood, What will happen in the dry?

From **Greenwood**

by Peter Yarrow

to record what happened to a community, but we do have anecdotal information from news accounts. In El Salvador, for example, we know that community continues to be torn by the knowledge that hundreds on both sides of the civil war committed atrocities. In Eastern Europe and republics of the former Soviet Union, community is being shredded by continuing discoveries of neighbors and friends who were informers for the secret police.

As community fails in one country or region, it has implications for other countries and regions. Now as desperate people from Eastern Europe, Asia, Africa, and Latin America attempt to relocate, they find they are not welcome in other lands. Over the 1984 to 1992 period, the number of people seeking asylum in Western Europe leaped from 100 thousand per year to 700 thousand people per year, a sevenfold increase in eight years. In response, asylum-granting procedures slowed and now stretch over seven years in Germany. Most applications are now rejected. Smugglers now transport not only illegal materials but also people into the Nordic countries.[46] The costs to Western European Governments of caring for the applicants and those rejected but not deported totaled $8.3 billion in 1992.[47]

The problem, of course, is not limited to Western Europe. Refugees are trying to escape from persecution, environmental deterioration, and economic collapse wherever they occur throughout the world. Desperate people are now willing to sell themselves into what amounts to slavery. Women have a particularly difficult time, and many are being driven to prostitution, even as young as eight years old.[48]

Another measure of the deterioration of community is provided by what is not in our news reports. In spite of the fact that 40,000 infants and children die each day of hunger[49] and complications of malnutrition, starving children are not featured in the evening news programs or on the front page. After decades, they are no longer "news."

Increasingly in the industrialized North and among the wealthy classes of the South, the poor are thought of as "them," somehow different from "us." The focus shifts from love and compassion to distancing and objectifying, to valuing anything that keeps "us" from being like "them."[50]

But as Buddhist monk Thích Nhât Hanh has noted, this shift to objectifying is not a realistic model:

[L]ook at wealth and poverty. The affluent society and the society deprived of everything inter-are. The wealth of one society is made of the poverty of the other. "This is like this, because that is like that." Wealth is made of non-wealth elements, and poverty is made of non-poverty elements...

We are not separate. We are inextricably interrelated. The rose is garbage, and the non-prostitute is the prostitute. The rich man is the very poor woman, and the Buddhist is the non-Buddhist. The non-Buddhist cannot help but be a Buddhist, because we inter-are. The emancipation of the young prostitute will come as she sees into the nature of inter-being. She will know that she is bearing the fruit of the whole world. And if we look into ourselves and see her, we bear her pain, and the pain of the whole world.[51]

To preserve and foster this sense of community that Thích Nhât Hanh calls "inter-are," we urgently need alternatives to despair and tragedy, and examples are emerging.[52] One is the city of Curitiba, the tenth-largest city in Brazil. Here, the mayor Jaime Lerner and the citizens of Curitiba have worked together to produce a first-world city in the third world.

Mayor Lerner, an architect turned political leader, builds community while thinking small and cheap. Subways, for example, do not appeal to him because they are expensive and time consuming to build. Using tube-shaped loading platforms and special buses, Lerner has built a municipal transit system as efficient as a subway. The tube stations are elevated so that people walk directly into the bus rather than up steps. Passengers pay their fares at turnstiles on entering the tube station rather than on entering the bus. People board at two per second, eight times as fast as on a conventional bus. Selected streets are reserved for buses, and as a result, buses travel at an average of 32 km/h (20 m.p.h.) and can transport more than three times as many people per day as conventional buses.

Another key to the mass transit system is integration of all modes of transport—cars, buses, trains, streetcars, boats, and bicycles. A 90-mile bike path offers an attractive alternative to motorized transport and has become a vital part of the city's transportation system.

Only two decades ago, the city had just 0.46 sq. m. (5 sq. ft.) of open space per person. Now, Curitiba has 51 sq. m. (550 sq. ft.) per person—three and a half times as much as New York City. Lerner feels that parks and high quality public transport give dignity to citizens and encourage them to take responsibility for helping with other problems.

And help they do. Over 20 years, 1.5 million trees have been planted. Seventy percent of the people regularly participate in the recycling program. Vouchers for surplus food encourage slum dwellers to bring in and recycle trash. Recovering alcoholics and homeless men work the trash sorting lines. Small businesses adopt street children. There is community.[53]

Like Mayor Lerner, Iceland's President Vigdis Finnbogadottir listens to the people and motivates them. When she became president of this largely deforested island, she announced that the people must bring their children to all of her speeches. Now after each speech, she and the children go out together to plant three trees: one for the girls, one for the boys, and one for the unborn. After she leaves, the girls must care for their trees, the boys for theirs, and together the girls and boys must care for the tree for the unborn.[54]

Another model is provided by the Salvadoran Center for Appropriate Technology (CESTA) in San Salvador. Dr. Ricardo Navarro, an ecologist and engineer, left a university position to form CESTA, which focuses on bringing technology to the service of people and on bringing peace to a community divided by a brutal civil war.

To bring technology to the people, CESTA operates a school to teach people how to build and repair bicycles and pedal-powered tools, such as the bici-taxi, bici-mill, bici-compressor, bici-garbage collector, and bici-carts. They also produce wheelchairs for the many maimed in the war. "El Salvador will never have enough gasoline to give everybody a car, so what we need are bicycles and pedal-powered tools," says Dr. Navarro.

Another technology CESTA promotes is composting latrines. "For our people to stay healthy, we need clean, non-polluting latrines. We have a fiesta and teach communities how to build latrines that are affordable and work well for years."

Although the war has stopped, peace has not yet returned between the Armed Forces and the Farabundo Martí National Liberation Front (FLMN). As a step toward peace, Dr. Navarro and his colleagues at CESTA have begun planting the Forest of Reconciliation on Guazapa Mountain. The goal is to plant one tree for each of the 75,000 soldiers, FLMN fighters, and civilians killed in the war. With each tree is the name, photograph, and a paragraph about the person honored. In the forest, there are no ideological divisions; trees remembering National Guard troops, FLMN members, and civilians grieve together all over the mountain.

The Reconciliation Forest provides conciliatory honors forever for all fallen, and especially for Archbishop Oscar Arnulfo Romero for whom the first tree—a chestnut—was planted. The Forest also contributes to the ecological restoration of Guazapa Mountain, which was severely damaged in the war.

Each of us must fight poverty, violence, and hatred that destroy the community and create despair. Like Adupa, we must insist on keeping our love. Humans cannot live without the resources of love and community.

CHOICES AND AN UNCERTAIN FUTURE

Earth has reached a fork in the path to the future. Down one path is a tragic wasteland. The climate has become hotter than today; floods and droughts are more frequent and more violent. Massive amounts of soil have washed into the sea. Most forests are gone. A large fraction of Earth's species are extinct, and the remaining ones are being lost rapidly. Oil and natural gas are gone.

Nine-tenths of the human population lives in hopeless poverty. Education and health services are gone. Economic, environmental, and moral decay spread uncontrollably. Ever wider areas cease to have any semblance of social order. Ethnic and religious rivalries fuel hatred, corruption, atrocities, and warfare. Many more children die in infancy from childhood diseases and malnutrition. AIDS, tuberculosis, and hunger kill adults so fast the bodies cannot be dealt with. Hope lies only in migration to other less crowded, less ecologically disrupted countries.

One-tenth of the human population ignores what is happening to the nine-tenths. The one-tenth attempts to maintain a rich, consumptive, industrialized economy by using military forces to obtain foreign resources (especially coal and uranium), to slow the migration of refugees, to slow drug trafficking and to counter terrorist attacks.[55]

A few individuals scattered around the world live in great opulence, supported by a vastly increased dependence of the industrialized populations on crack cocaine and other drugs.

Down the other path is a very different Earth. A just, sustainable development for the whole Earth has become the principal goal of every nation and people. The peoples are united in planet-wide efforts to understand Earth and its peoples and to envision what Earth and its peoples can become. Protection of Earth has become a top priority for every person. Human ignorance, poverty, and bigotry are recognized everywhere as primary threats to national security and the future of Earth. Living conditions on the whole planet are comparable with the average level that existed in Europe in 1990.[56]

None of us wants to go down the path to the tragic wasteland. We all want a very different kind of future for ourselves, our children, and our grandchildren. How can we avoid the tragic wasteland and reach a just, sustainable future? What follows is a sampling of suggestions from several sources:[57]

FOR THE CHILDREN

The rising hills,
the slopes,
of statistics lie before us.
the steep climb
of everything, going up,
up, as we all go down.

In the next century
or the one beyond that,
they say,
are valley, pastures,
we can meet there
in peace
if we make it.

To climb these
coming crests
one word to you,
to you and
your children:

stay together
learn the flowers
go light

Gary Snyder

Turtle Island

- to recognize that a sustainable, just, and healthy human development requires as its first condition a sustainable, just, and healthy human relationship with Earth;

- to create everywhere the social, economic, political, religious, and legal conditions necessary to reduce human fertility to replacement levels or below;

- to reduce significantly the per capita use of both source resources (oil, gas, rich mineral ores, forests, etc.) and sink resources (disposal space in the atmosphere and oceans) by the wealthiest individuals and nations;

- to create national economies everywhere capable of providing basic education, primary health care, and civil order and justice for everyone;

- to modify the agricultural, forestry, and urbanization practices across the planet to preserve arable soils;

- to double agricultural yields while reducing the dependence of agricultural systems on fossil fuels, the contamination of ground and surface waters with fertilizers and pesticides, and the creation of agricultural pests through the use of pesticides;

- to provide orderly transition from carbon dioxide emitting energy sources (oil, coal, fuelwood) to a highly efficient, renewable, and non-polluting energy economy that is affordable for even the poorest;

- to cut the emissions of all greenhouse gases to eliminate the prospect of highly disruptive changes in climatic conditions and the levels of the world's oceans;

- to eliminate everywhere by 2000 the emissions of chlorofluorocarbons and other chemicals now destroying the ozone layer in the stratosphere;

- to find and employ alternatives to war, violence, and militarism in resolving differences among nations and peoples; and

- to keep alive hope, love, and compassion and to build relationships of trust and cooperation that will allow us all to get through the difficult times ahead with a minimum of violence, hatred, and despair.

While North and South are both integral parts of a single planet, their situations are so different that it has frequently been difficult for them to work constructively together. Nonetheless, there are several actions that must be undertaken cooperatively by the North and South. Together North and South must:

- use the opportunity afforded by the end of the Cold War to build a just and equitable new world order. New participatory mechanisms must be designed to replace those designed for the Cold War era (for example, the U.N. Security Council);

- promote education, information and democracy, which are the things that make nations different now and that can make the whole world different in the 21st century;

- make development peace. Over the past 40 years capital transfers from the North to South have not been as successful as planned, and there has been a tendency for unproductive finger-pointing on both sides. It would be much more useful to acknowledge that the transfers could have been more successful but for:

  - the pursuit in both the North and South of an unsustainable development model that ignored the fact that the human economy is embedded in a finite biosphere;

  - a sometimes desperate need of Northern banks to lend to the South;

  - excessive and preemptive use by the North of global source and sink resources needed by the South;

  - flawed governmental policies in the South promoting (a) mislocated, inefficient industries; (b) misallocation of capital, including government expenditures; (c) support of the interests of affluent urban elites, the large (and often corrupt) governmental bureaucracy, and the military at the expense of peasant agriculture;

  - the failure of the South to establish policies that consistently make family limitation advantageous to couples and make safe and affordable contraceptives readily available;

  - abuse of military, political, and economic power by the North to obtain access to Southern resources at unreasonably low prices; and

- continuation in the South of social systems that doom three-fourths of the population, especially women and low social classes, to an unproductive and stagnating existence.

- shore up the feeling that it is possible for international norms to bring a just and equitable peace to world affairs. A strong, clear, non-discriminatory body of international law is urgently needed, as are confidence-building measures to improve international participation and break the mold of the old discriminatory international system. The strengthening of international law and the rule of law is essential to restore the global political confidence that will permit action;

- establish a continuing forum for global discussions of the whole human mega problem, the global problematique, and renegotiate the terms upon which nations communicate with each other. The agenda must cease to be limited to a few narrow topics and be opened to embrace in an orderly way everything each nation (whether developing or industrialized) fears. Only by opening up the agenda can we reconceptualize and begin to deal with the nature of threats to national and global security, the reality of economic and ecologic interdependence, and the design of participatory, cooperative solutions;

- reinforce positive values in the international community, values such as dignified self-reliance and independence, and acknowledgment of developmental needs such as participatory democracy, the guaranteeing of international law on the basis of equality and principle (rather than on the basis of force), and above all, solidarity;

- replace the outmoded and misleading U.N. System of National Accounts (UNSNA) with a new set of national indicators that provide a yardstick for measuring the degree to which a nation is living sustainably within its own source and sink resources;

- expand the negotiations under the General Agreement on Trade and Tariffs (GATT) to address how international trade can become a force for sustainable development and protection of the global environment;

- assess the current global agricultural research agenda in terms of its ability to lead to a sustainable and secure global food supply that is profitable for the world's farmers and affordable for the world's poorest;

- establish everywhere social and institutional conditions that actively resist corruption and favoritism by making opportunities for upward social mobility dependent on personal contribution rather than on class, cultural, or religious background or on race or gender; and

- accelerate the transfer of up-to-date, socially and environmentally beneficial technologies, especially technologies for: processing raw materials efficiently into value-added products, generating renewable energy, conserving energy, water, and other resources, providing safe and effective contraception, preventing waste and pollution, recycling, furthering agricultural systems that are low-input, organic, and recycling of nutrients, and reducing the material- and energy-intensity of manufacturing.

Some essential actions can only be taken by the North and some only be done by the South.

The North should:

- make its primary contribution to global sustainability by stabilizing its resource consumption and reducing its direct and indirect damage to the global life-support systems of Earth. People living in the North must become aware of their addiction to consumerism, to never having enough wealth, property, and "things," and to careers of advancement and power. Northerners must find a grander meaning for their lives than consumerism and power. They must learn how their lifestyles and expectations deplete the resources needed by the South. Generally, Northerners live well enough that they do not need to increase their incomes and use of global resources. But Northerners do need to address domestic poverty and homelessness, a major disgrace in some Northern countries;

- provide international debt relief by: (a) canceling or writing off those debts that accelerate the liquidation of natural capital, fail to internalize the full costs of pollution, are clearly unsustainable, or are inherently not repayable; (b) addressing the current imbalance between commercial rate loans, subsidized investments, and grants to the South; and (c) improving the relative proportions of the Northern transfers as loans, subsidized or concessionary arrangements, or grants;

- accelerate its transition to a renewable energy economy. To do this it will be necessary to include the environmental costs of non-renewable energy supplies in the price consumers pay. For example, there needs to be a "carbon tax" on all energy derived from oil, gas, and coal reflecting the cost to Earth of the carbon dioxide released by the use of these fuels;

- internalize the costs of disposal of its toxic and other wastes within its own borders. Even if the countries of the South have a "comparative advantage" in being "under-polluted," the countries of the North should not be shipping waste to the South;

- use "defense" funds to invest in the South. If the countries of the North used some of their enormous military budgets to reduce poverty and protect the local (and global) environment in the South, it would improve conditions in the South, reduce desperation and the willingness to engage in acts of terrorism, and thereby reduce Northern feelings of insecurity; and

- acknowledge that the wealth and strength of the economies and military forces of the North have been achieved in part through the preemptive use of the planet's limited resources, including both source resources and sink resources. Then, engage in negotiations with the South on suitable reparation payments for historically disproportionate preemption of the global resources.

The South should:

- make its primary contribution to global sustainability by achieving population stability. For this to happen government policies must change consistently from pro-natalist to anti-natalist and consistent laws and policies must be established to make family limitation strongly advantageous for couples and to make large families highly disadvantageous. It will be necessary to:

- make formal education (primary and secondary) compulsory—especially for girls—and effectively enforce attendance;

  - outlaw child labor even within family-owned businesses;

  - place on parents the major financial responsibility for raising their own children, including education and health care;

  - give women access to income-earning opportunities in the labor market, including jobs not easily compatible with childbearing and childrearing;

- maintain and strengthen family planning programs, giving attention to ensuring that contraceptives are safe, effective, affordable;

- provide effective legal guarantees of property rights and legal enforcement of private contracts; and

- develop private and public insurance and pension programs that are reliable and attractive, thus offering an alternative to children as a source of old age security;

- pursue poverty alleviation through: (a) employment and self-reliance strategies using local resources to produce for domestic needs, (b) value-added processing of resources, and (c) microloan programs for women;

- engage in direct poverty alleviation through: (a) programs that include social safety nets and targeted aid, and (b) the use of foreign exchange both from loans and exports to serve the needs of the poor more than the desires of the rich;

- give emphasis to "human capital" formation through education, training, and employment creation, particularly for girls and women;

- replace, as soon as possible, "throughput growth" (as measured by GDP) with growth by productivity improvements as the path of progress;

- accelerate its transition to renewable energy by internalizing environmental costs in energy prices and phasing in carbon and non-renewable energy taxes;

- recognize that the North's past "damage the environment and then cure it" approach has proved to be enormously expensive and unwise. The "prevention approach" is probably the only strategy that is affordable for the South. In particular, the South should prevent, to the fullest extent possible, irreversible environmental losses, especially loss of biodiversity and losses of soils. These are the true "non-renewable" resources of a nation because these resources, once gone, cannot be replaced at any cost; and

- bypass the technologies used in the North's environmentally damaging stage of economic evolution and choose instead the most up-to-date technologies to conserve energy and other resources, prevent pollution, and create (rather than eliminate) jobs.

How much time do we have to do these things? There is no precise answer to this question. It is like we are walking down a slippery path that is becoming steeper and more slippery with every step. Steps we have already taken have produced needless suffering, hatred, and irreparable ecological damage, but if we turn now we can avoid much further suffering and damage. If we keep on our present course much longer, there will come a time when we will inevitably slip and slide uncontrollably into global disaster.

The signs are all around us. Every year of delay in stabilizing population growth adds 90 million children to the human population, most of whom are not receiving adequate nutrition, education, and health care. Every year we delay developing the post-petroleum energy economy we burn 20 billion barrels of our declining petroleum resource and increase the risk of planet-wide disruptions of commercial energy supplies. Every year we delay protecting the habitat of endangered species leads to another 30,000 extinctions. Every year of delay in developing alternative technologies for increasing agricultural yields places the food supply of our children and grandchildren in further jeopardy. Every year we delay in stabilizing greenhouse gas emissions commits the world to more global warming and a greater rise in the sea level.

All of us have had the experience of stopping. When walking, we can stop in seconds, in a step or two at most. Many of us have ridden a bicycle, and we know that it takes a bit longer to stop a bicycle. Many of us, too, have driven an automobile, and the delay between applying the brakes and coming to a stop has led to many collisions and injuries. Fewer of us have ever tried to stop a small truck loaded with a ton of cargo, or a large truck loaded with several tons. Very few of us here ever tried to stop a 100-car train fully loaded with coal or iron ore. Almost none of us has tried to stop a fully loaded supertanker, which has so much momentum that 10 miles are required to stop. But even the momentum of a supertanker is trivial compared to the momentum inherent in the current unsustainable growth in human numbers and human consumption, and we humans have never even tested the brakes on these huge, complex global systems. Even now, the momentum of these systems will carry them to much destruction and tragedy. If we humans are to stop short of an enormously destructive collision with reality, we must act very soon. We do not have decades or generations to spare. If we take the "braking" actions described above within the next five to ten years, the land we need to meet human needs (see Figure 21) would probably approach but not exceed the land available, and a sustainable future for Earth would be possible.

The Real Problem

The actions described on the preceding pages are daunting. They require extraordinary engineering and management skills and extraordinary creativity and inventiveness. Demanding as the economic, engineering, and management tasks are, there is yet a still more difficult matter: the many barriers to the necessary political action.[58]

1. There are areas of uncertainty about the nature of the ecological crisis we face, and some people seize upon these uncertainties as excuses

The awful truth remains that a large part of humanity will suffer no matter what is done.

E. O. Wilson

"Is Humanity Suicidal?"

The New York Times

Magazine. *30 May 1993.*

p. 24.

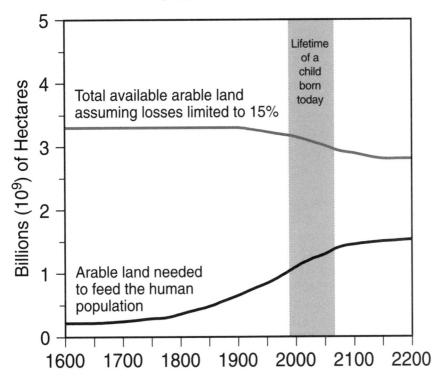

A Sustainable Future

Figure 21: *The sustainable future: Arable land needed to feed the human population assuming agricultural yields double, population does not exceed 12 billion, and losses of arable land are limited to 15 percent.*

Before me, beauty.
Behind me, beauty.
Below me, beauty.
Above me, beauty.
Around me, beauty.
May I speak beauty.
May I walk in beauty always.
Beauty I am.
All is restored to beauty.
All is restored to beauty.
All is restored to beauty.
All is restored to beauty.

Navajo

for inaction. Most well informed physical and social scientists today agree that we face an ecological crisis without any precedent in historical times. Those who, for the purpose of maintaining balance in debate, take the contrary view that there is significant uncertainty about whether it is real are hurting our ability to respond.

2. There is an instinctive unwillingness to believe that something so far outside the bounds of historical experience can, in fact, be occurring. The trends presented in this report, for example, have not been absorbed and owned by many people, and as a result, they assume the trends can't be real.

3. There is a human tendency, encouraged by some faith traditions, toward exceptionalism, which holds that humankind so intelligent and so spirited that, as a species, we are not bound by ecological laws as other species are. Exceptionalists in several faith traditions believe that no matter how serious the problem, the ingenuity and sheer will of the human species—combined with divine dispensation—will produce a solution.

4. There is an assumption made by many that it will be easier and more sensible to adapt to whatever change occurs than it will be to prevent the crisis. Unfortunately, changes of the magnitude and complexity that seems likely can come so swiftly that adaptation is essentially impossible. The collapse of the Soviet Union is just one small reminder of how seemingly large, stable systems can change very quickly.

5. There is the lack of widespread awareness among the peoples of the world about the nature of the global problematique. Many spiritual leaders, many political leaders, and much of the general public are unaware of what is happening and how serious it is.

6. There is also the knowledge among those few who do know what is happening and how severe it is that the solutions are harder than anything we humans have done before. A redirection of much of our science and technology would be required. Our economies would have to be largely redesigned. Why try, especially when it may all come to naught anyway?

In addition to these six barriers to action, there is a seventh of overriding importance: Our shared moral basis for a sustained, cooperative effort—

our development model—has failed. We are now a people—a species—without a vision. This is our *real* problem.

Our current development model begins with the assumption that all that is—Earth, the solar system, all stars, and beyond was created for us, the human species. The non-human part of Earth, "nature," is specifically for use of the human species in any way humans see fit. Nature is a "resource" for all human use.

Nature, however, is dangerous. In our relationship to nature, we humans are vulnerable to death and disease and must work for food and shelter. This vulnerability in which we live in nature is termed the "human condition."

Most humans have long resented their condition vis-a-vis nature. Plato began a conceptual separation of human and the non-human. But it was the millennial vision of John of Patmos and its secular interpretation in the industrial West generally and especially in the United States that stirred in humans the thought of something better.

In his Book of Revelation in the Christian Bible, John of Patmos foresaw (see chapters 20 and 21) a period of a thousand years during which Christians, through their faith, will rise above the human condition, immune to the dangers of nature. In his words: "...and death shall be no more, neither shall there be mourning nor crying nor pain anymore..."[59]

Gradually, the millennial dream began to be seen not as a spiritual state, but as a physical condition to be achieved by human control over nature. Francis Bacon (1561-1626) accelerated this shift in thinking by arguing that the human species not only could gain control over nature but should make doing so the primary goal of the human species. The Western concept of "development" is essentially a secularized version of the millennial dream: a rising above the human condition not through spiritual development, but through ruthless control and manipulation of nature.[60]

The principal instrument through which humans seek development and progress is the institution called the nation-state. Groups of humans have marked off areas of Earth as their own "nation," and each nation has declared itself "sovereign," i.e., an independent entity subject to no other power on Earth.[61]

Through their respective nations, groups of humans attempt to rise above the human condition through "development." Development means using capital equipment, technological knowledge of nature, and non-human energy sources to replace human labor in providing human food and shelter. It also means destroying species that compete with humans for food-producing habitat or that pose a threat to human life and safety. And finally, it means achieving security against other groups of humans—other nations—through violence or the threat of violence.

Nations developed a variety of subsidiary institutions, the most important being corporations, the military, and schools. Elaborate rules (laws) govern the behavior of individuals and institutions within nations.

Corporations proved to be particularly important to nations as a means of accumulating capital. Corporations are "fictitious persons," institutions able to do virtually anything a person can do—own property, enter into contracts, hire and fire employees, and even reproduce—and motivated through fiduciary responsibility to maximize return on stockholders' investments. Unlike real persons, corporations have no biological need for clean air, safe water, non-toxic food, and other environmental conditions, and the liability of stockholders for damages and injuries caused by the corporation is limited. Corporations have proven to be effective accumulators of capital, and many now are larger economically than small nation-states. As they have grown in economic power, corporations have become increasingly difficult for nation-states to control or regulate.

Most major faith traditions have generally accepted the legitimacy of the reigning development model—the whole collection of assumptions, theories, and institutions described above. Those few faith traditions that have not accepted the legitimacy of the reigning development model have been unable to make a thorough and effective criticism.

Nonetheless, the reigning development model has failed. It is being rejected now both by humans and by Earth.

As far as humans are concerned, the legitimacy of the reigning development model rested primarily on the assumption that the model was inherently equitable and replicable among nations. Disparities in the human conditions found in different nations were assumed not to be a result of an inequity inherent in the development model or the resulting system of nation-states and corporations, but in the lack of intelligence and tenacity among those humans living in the "poorer" parts of the world. It was not unjust that some nations have large pieces of the global economic pie, because if the people of other nations were simply diligent, they could make their piece of the pie as large as they like. The total pie could be arbitrarily large.

This foundation of legitimacy has crumbled to dust. For the people of the South to live as the people in the North now live would require an increase by a factor of five to ten in the total economic activity on the planet.[62] Few who have reflected on the matter feel that the source and sink resources of the planet could sustain such a large increase in the total economic activity. So, the reigning model fails because it is neither equitable[63] nor replicable for all nations.[64]

The model fails from the human perspective for another reason: it has left half of the human population—the female half—outside of progress. The reigning model embraces and perpetuates all of the "patriarchal" institutions: the nation-state, the modern corporation, and the ecclesiastical hierarchies of several faith traditions. Under these institutions, invented by and still governed by men, most women in the world are born into cradle-to-grave oppression, discrimination, and poverty with no possibility of escape. All across a planet controlled by patriarchal institutions, girls are fed less, pulled out of school earlier, forced into hard labor sooner, and given less care than boys, as has been demonstrated by study after study.[65] There is no legitimacy to a development model that perpetuates institutions oppressing half of humanity.

Finally, Earth itself rejects the model. The non-human part of Earth is not for humans to "own," use, and abuse any way they please. Nation-states are not independent entities subject to no other power on Earth. The human economy is only a part of a much larger, but still finite, global biosphere, and the human economy cannot flourish if the biosphere does not flourish. The human destiny and the destiny of Earth are inseparably linked. Any development theory that begins with a different premise is fundamentally flawed.

The Task Ahead

The first principle of the new model must be that humans and Earth be in a mutually enhancing relationship. Without this principle as a starting point, no model of development, no vision of progress is sustainable.

The task ahead is to rethink our model of development, our vision of what we and Earth can become, and our concept of progress.

This is a large task, as has been explained well by Father Thomas Berry:

> *This task concerns every member of the human community, no matter what the occupation, continent, ethnic group, or age. It is a task from which no one is absolved and with which no one is ultimately more concerned than anyone else. Here we meet as absolute equals to face our ultimate tasks as human beings within the life systems of the planet Earth. We have before us the question not simply of physical survival, but of survival in a human mode of being, survival and development into intelligent, affectionate, imaginative persons thoroughly enjoying the universe about us.... It is a question...of a concern that reaches out to all the living and nonliving beings of the earth and in some manner out to the distant stars in the heavens.*[66]

The task ahead is to reexamine, reconsider, and reformulate every human institution to ensure that it fosters and supports our first principle: a mutually enhancing relationship between the human species and Earth as an unavoidable necessity for mutually enhancing relationships among humans. The institutions in question include international organizations, nation-states, domestic and multinational corporations, the family, and the faith traditions.

The nation-state system of international organization began in 1648. It was the time of collapse of the Holy Roman Empire and the signing of the Peace of Westphalia. At that time, the concept of sovereignty made sense, but then the global issues of "development," nuclear war, and climate change were not yet in anyone's mind.[67]

The original international organization was the League of Nations, created by nation-states after World War I. It was to have prevented further world wars. After World War II, the League of Nations was replaced by the United Nations system of international organizations, again to prevent world war.

With the end of the world Cold War, the U.N. system needs to be completely reexamined in terms of the needs of the 21st century. A principal need of the 21st century will be a global institution speaking to nations about the need for a mutually enhancing relationship between the human species (and its various national groupings) and Earth. The U.N., as it currently functions, is not well-suited to this task,[68] and Secretary General Boutros Boutros-Ghali is encouraging some major institutional reforms by 1995, the 50th anniversary of the U.N.

The premise of "sovereignty" underlying modern nation-states is false. Nations are not independent entities subject to no other power on Earth. They are all interdependent and very much subject to the health and welfare of the entire ecosystem of Earth, of which they are but a modest part. The imaginary lines around nations, the "borders," generally have no relationship to the boundaries of watersheds, airsheds, and other natural systems and complicate the development of mutually enhancing Earth- human relationships. The rules (laws) nations establish to govern human and institutional behavior within their borders are generally based on the assumption that the non-human part of Earth is simply a "resource" of no value until "used" by humans.

Nation-states must change radically. Nations now do absolutely appalling things to their own people, to other nations, and to Earth. Within a few decades, the fallacious notion of sovereignty must disappear and be replaced with an understanding that "nations" (or whatever name we give to the institutions that replace nation-states) are all intimately inter-connected with each other and with Earth. Laws that implicitly assume the non-human part of Earth to be merely a "resource" must all be replaced. Gross National Product, the reigning measure of development of a nation, must be replaced with indicators that measure the sustain-ability of the human-Earth relationship within the nation's boundaries.

Relationships between nations will require major revision. Trade, migra-tion, and the use of global-commons sources and sinks must all be reconsidered from the standpoint of the equity of patterns of interac-tion, sustainability, and replicability and of an overall mutually enhanc-ing human-Earth relationship.

The assumed right of nations to wage war requires total reconsideration. Wars, especially with modern nuclear, chemical, and biological weapons, do not promote a mutually enhancing human-Earth relationship, and the intellectual talent, money, and physical resources are urgently needed for other purposes. Since peoples will probably always kill as a last resort to protect themselves and their children, it may not be possible to eliminate war entirely. However, there must be more attention to ways of resolving inter-nation, ethnic, religious, and sectional disputes short of war.

Alternatives to war are beginning to be discussed internationally. "Preventive diplomacy" and "new dispute resolution techniques" have been proposed by U.S. Secretary of State Warren Christopher to keep conflicts from spreading. Some diplomats are beginning to suggest that the international community may have the right to intervene in a country simply because that country is mistreating its minority groups. Another possibility is an international tribunal to hear the claims of aggrieved minorities in countries, a responsibility beyond that of the International Court of Justice, which is limited to adjudicating claims between countries. Others are openly suggesting that states incapable of governing themselves be taken over by force and placed under U.N. Trusteeship, thus making the United Nations a new colonial power.[69]

But perhaps we need a level of globally accepted means of international challenge that stops short of war. The quintessential image of people willing to die, but not kill, for their country is Mahatma Gandhi's men marching peacefully on the British Dharsana Salt Works in May 1930 where rank after rank after rank were brutally clubbed down by four hundred Surat policemen under the command of British officers.[70] The concept of non-violent, citizen-based defense has been seriously proposed by Professor Gene Sharp of The Center for International Affairs, Harvard University, and by Mexico's Sr. Caridad Inda, chair of the Center. Together with others they have founded the Association for Transarmament Studies and published a how-to-do-it book on citizen-based defense.[71]

Multinational corporations have become global institutions, in some cases largely beyond the political control of nation-states. Although corporations are chartered by and theoretically under the control of nation-states, they could become much more powerful in the future, perhaps eventually replacing nation-states as the principal institutional form of global organization. Although some corporate leaders are showing an awareness of the need for corporations—as well as human beings—to be in a mutually enhancing relationship with Earth,[72] the fiduciary responsibilities of corporate leaders to their stockholders limit the actions they can take. In theory, control of a corporation rests largely with the political entity that grants the corporation its charter or approves its articles of incorporation. This authority has shifted over the years from the nation-state to provinces, and there is much competition among chartering political entities to attract corporations (and the tax base and jobs they create) by readily granting corporate charters and imposing few restraints on what corporations can do.

In the United States, at least one organization (Charter, Ink.)(sic) is attempting to increase citizen control of corporations by asking chartering governments to strengthen the laws governing corporations and by initiating campaigns and legal proceedings to take back the charters of particularly offensive corporations.[73] To be effective, however, such efforts must be made on a global basis. The laws defining fictitious corporate persons need to be strengthened in a coordinated way throughout the world. Soon, within a decade or two at most, corporations throughout the world must be in a mutually enhancing relationship with Earth. Such a relationship is essential for the future of business because, ultimately, ecological destruction is bad even for business.

The family is the primary school for teaching values. It is in the family that we must learn the mutually enhancing Earth-human relationships that are necessary for mutually enhancing relationships among humans. It is in the family that our children learn from the example of their parents (and sometimes the parents from the children) the difference between needs and wants and the meaning of enough. It is also from the example of their parents that our children learn how men and women are to relate, how to be masculine or feminine, and how large a family is appropriate and desirable. And it is here that our children are guided into a faith tradition and taught either to hate, disparage, and shun or to love, appreciate, and accept those who are different in faith, culture, and race.

THE ROLE OF FAITH TRADITIONS

We humans have begun asking questions about "sustainable development." This is an important question, but it does not go deep enough. We must also begin asking questions about "sustainable faith."

Is there a faith tradition in existence today that is practicing a way of life that provides "progress" for the whole community of life, not just the human species? Is there a faith tradition such that if everyone on Earth suddenly adopted it, the human future on Earth would be assured?

I do not know enough about the faith traditions of the world to provide a well-considered answer to this question, but on the basis of my limited personal experience, I doubt that there is a faith tradition on Earth today that can provide the moral foundation needed for the 21st century.

Specifically, I do not believe my own faith, Christianity, is a sustainable faith—at least not as it is generally understood and practiced. The Bible, especially the New Testament, is a weak document on the subject of mutually enhancing human-Earth relations. Admittedly, there are a few scattered texts in the Bible (especially the Old Testament) that suggest "stewardship" of resources and concern for the land:

- Is it not enough for you to drink the clear water? Must you also muddy the rest with your feet? (Ezek. 34:18)

- Woe to you who add house to house and join field to field, till no space is left and you live alone in the land. (Isaiah 5:8)

- Take with you... every kind of...animal...to keep their various kinds alive throughout the earth. (Gen. 7:3)

- I brought you into a fertile land to eat its fruit and rich produce. But you came and defiled my land and made my inheritance detestable. (Jer. 2:7)

- The time has come...for destroying those who destroy the earth. (Revel. 11:18)

But if gathered together, such texts would scarcely cover a single page of the Bible. There is no unequivocal commandment, "Thou shalt not destroy Earth." Furthermore, the only biblical guidance on the stewardship of the gift of human fertility is: "Be fruitful and multiply" (Gen.

1:28), and such limited and inappropriate guidance on this critical matter is not adequate for a sustainable faith.*

To make matters worse, the institutional manifestations of Christianity have shown little or no serious interest in a mutually enhancing human-Earth relationship. With perhaps a few exceptions, churches are not prime examples of excellent stewardship of resources; they are generally as wasteful and environmentally thoughtless as any other human institution. Churches have no active environmental programs comparable with secular environmental groups. Churches do not use effectively what limited environmental guidance the Bible provides. The few Earth-sensitive texts in the Bible (such as those above) are not in the lectionary and as a result are almost never the subject of sermons and homilies. Seminaries teach the Bible, church history, theology, inter-human ethics, and homiletics, but do not provide even primer-level knowledge of Earth or inter-species ethics. Budgets and most major statements[74] by Christian churches lack commitment and substance on human relations with Earth.

Why is this? The God I know cares a great deal about Earth and is not at all pleased with what we humans are doing to Earth and to each other. Why then is the sacred text of my faith such a weak source of inspiration and guidance on caring for Earth and on the stewardship of the gift of human fertility?

Personally, I suspect it is because the early Christian community understood that the second coming of Christ would be very soon, within their generation. They delayed decades before writing the gospels probably thinking Christ would return so soon that it would not be necessary to write for future generations. Three hundred years later, Christ had not returned, but at the Council of Nicea Christians closed their sacred text, the Bible, confident that they had all the revelation needed until Christ's return.

Now 1700 years later there still has been no second coming of Christ, and there have been no further revelations added to our sacred text to

---

* In 1991 the member churches of the World Council of Churches have resolved to encourage each other to "[d]evelop and implement educational programs . . . , both in churches and in other communities, on matters related to environmental and ecological concerns. *This should include the matter of responsible stewardship of human fertility ....*"[75] (Emphasis added.)

guide us in addressing the issues of the 21st century. We do have some "church tradition" that has evolved over the centuries, but it is not particularly helpful in dealing with many of the issues before us. I wonder if God has stopped speaking to us, or if we have stopped listening.*

Sir Shridath Ramphal, former Secretary General of the Commonwealth and Foreign Minister of Guyana, has implicitly raised this same question in the context of "the holy texts of many religions." He writes as follows in the official report prepared for the opening the United Nations Conference on Environment and Development:

> *In the language of the Independent Commission on International Humanitarian Issues..., the holy texts of many religions, not to mention legal traditions, philosophies, and custom "... abound in moral injunctions that imply an ethic of human solidarity... For centuries, the great religious texts*

---

* Some of my fellow Christians have reviewed drafts of the previous paragraphs and expressed some discomfort and dissatisfaction. They have asked that I identify my specific Christian affiliation (Protestant, and more specifically, Lutheran) and to acknowledge that my observations on Christianity are on the basis of my personal experience (which I do acknowledge).

Some Christian reviewers have also taken exception to my assertion that all of the Christian scriptures addressing a mutually enhancing human-Earth relationship "would scarcely cover a single page of the Bible." In support of their position, they refer to the following parts of the Bible: Gen. 1 and 2 "properly exegeted," 8:22; 9:8-17; Deut. 6:1-3; 8:7-10; Psalms 24:1-2; 50:10-12; 65:9-13; 96:10- 13; 104; 145; 146; 147; 148; Is. 40-55; 65:17-25; Hos. 2:18-20; 4:1-3; Matt. 6:26-30; 12:11-12; Luke 12:6-7, 24-25; 15:4-7; Rom. 8:18-23; Ephes. 1:9-10; Col. 1:15-20; John 1:1-14.

While I admit that these passages would not fit on one page, I find the guidance given them is not as direct, unambiguous, and specific, as I and many friends and colleagues would wish and does indeed need to be "properly exegeted." Inferences can be drawn from these and other parts of the Bible about human-Earth and Earth-God relations, but what little unambiguous and direct guidance there is would probably fit on less than one page. On the whole the Bible seems to me focused on human-human and human-God relations, not on human-Earth or even Earth-God relationships, and none of the several institutional manifestations of Christianity have been able to surmount this great weakness inherent in Christianity's sacred text, the Bible.

I am not arguing that Christians should abandon their faith in search of another (as one concerned reviewer thought I was), but only that the God I know—and I think it is the Christian God—is much more concerned about human-Earth relations and about the stewardship of the gift of human fertility than would be apparent to most readers of the Bible or to most observers of the institutional manifestations and traditions of Christianity. (continued...)

have taught the essential oneness of the human race." What scriptures have not always taught is that nature is the loom on which is woven life's seamless fabric of which humanity is a significant, but not unduly dominant, part.[76]

New Revelations

The God I know is still speaking,[77] and there have been at least four new revelations.

First, it has been revealed that among the most destructive forces on Earth today is hatred between the followers of different faith traditions. Of the fifty plus armed conflicts in progress currently, the majority are motivated in significant part by hatred of the followers of one faith for the followers of another faith.[78] The arms industry—the largest industry in the world, larger even than illegal drugs and oil—is supported in significant part by the hatred of the followers of one faith for the followers of another faith.

Stories of interreligious hatred and violence are found on page after page of our history books and now almost daily in our newspapers. There are

---

(...continued) For this reason, I think all forms of Christianity must open themselves increasingly to the possibility of further revelation and knowledge, especially on matters relating to human-Earth relations and the stewardship of the gift of human fertility.

Some Christian reviewers have objected that I undervalue the Christian concept of "stewardship of resources." In my view, a very serious part of the human problem is the Christian (or other) notion of "resources," something of Earth taken and given value when passed though the human economy and made "useful" to humans. The notion that parts of Earth are of no value unless of benefit to humans may derive from the Christian nation of "redeeming the whole creation." What can it mean to "redeem the non-human parts of the creation"?[79] Obviously, to assure that they serve their God-given purpose, which, in most Christian thinking, means to be of use to humans.[80] This wrong concept is central to much of western law concerning human-Earth relations and is especially destructive in the notion that the "highest and best use of land" is always to be desired and is always measured in terms of current human benefits. The Christian concept of "stewardship of resources" is inadequate and inappropriate because the Christian concept of "resource" denies any value to the non-human parts of Earth except to the extent that they benefit humans.

Finally, some Christian reviewers have objected that we are not trying to save "Earth." Earth they argue, will still be here even if the human species destroys itself. I disagree. Earth and its possibilities would be so immeasurably reduced and impoverished by the loss of the human species that it would no longer be Earth. In fact, it is even impossible to imagine Earth without humans.[81] The human destiny is inseparably linked to that of Earth, and we humans have become a bio-geo-chemical force reshaping Earth. The God I know wants us humans—one species—as a responsible co-creator of an Earth-future worthy of the original creator. Nothing less will do for me.

so many that it takes an extraordinary one to catch our attention. An extraordinary one appeared recently in the National Catholic Reporter under the headline "Torture, Rape, Murder Outlaw Love in Bosnia":

You ask me my name? So the entire world can witness my shame? Just write: female Muslim, 35 years old, professor of literature. As for my newborn son, I have simply given him the name Jihad. The first time I ever nursed him I said, "If you ever forget, may this milk curse you so help me God."

The Serbians have taught me to hate. For the last two months, within me I have only hatred, no pain or bitterness. Emptiness.

Not so long ago I taught my students only love. But my Serbian neighbor's only son, Zoran, who was also my pupil, urinated in my mouth. While wild-bearded vagabonds were roaring with laughter, Zoran told me: "You are good for nothing, you stinking Muslim woman."

I don't recall if I heard a scream or felt a blow to my body. This colleague, a physics professor who yelled like a maniac at me, began to beat me continuously. My mouth filled with blood.

There is nothing strange here; I have been deadened to the pain but my soul...it hurts, oh how it hurts so much. I taught my students to love, and they were preparing themselves, and even bringing up their children to slaughter all who are not Orthodox Christian. Jihad, war! As simple as that!

Our best man at our wedding was even a Serbian! Poor me and my people. Leave the fine words of love for someone else. You may talk about Muhammad and Muslim goodness as much as you wish. Even if I lose another eye, I will walk blind and curse every Muslim who speaks of "forgiveness."

You ask what they have done. They raped my mother before my eyes, my good—beyond beautiful—old mother.

I remember my childhood, the garden near the house, and my mother hesitating beneath the trees. She would seek the blossoms where the fragrance was most intense; she would spread the bed linen. Yes, she would bow to Allah and pray.

Wherever I turn now I smell my mother's fragrance. I wait for her footsteps, those soft, quiet steps and the rustling sounds from her Muslim robes.

I cannot forget the stench and roar of my neighbor Sava Pejic, whom my cousin once dated. As he jumped on my mother, I lost consciousness.

Blows to my body woke me. Her hand was still warm; lifeless, but warm. The heat still burns within me; so does regret, for just that same morning we quarreled. It was about Papa. She always worried about where he was.

That same day he had gone to his relatives in a village nearby, which saved his life, but not for long. People say when he heard about his wife he didn't cry. But he stood in silence all day. In the morning he was found hanging, facing the meadow where my mother saw him the very first time.

No, my husband doesn't know about our second child's birth and I don't know where he and my other son are. They assure me they are somewhere in Macedonia. What can I do? I have to believe if for the sake of Jihad.

Believe me, it's very hard to concentrate. They pulled me off from my dead mother and dragged me by my hair. They asked me, "Where is the gold?" Instinctively, I pointed at my pregnant stomach of eight months, but I suddenly remembered and I showed them.

On the way to headquarters in Vogosce, they spit on me and kicked me. I recognized the Duke of Chetniks, Jovan Tintor, who stood silent and watched. The others had been drinking. Tintor said, "Bring Janko!" He cut my hair so it formed a cross. On my hand with a knife he carved "S" (the sign of the Serbian Chetniks) four times.

"This is just the beginning if you don't tell us where the rest of your relatives are," Tintor yelled. They poured drinks over me and forced me to strip.

Nightmare was interrupted by the noise coming from the street. They took me outside, naked as I was. In the middle of the courtyard stood a girl. She was less than 10 years old. Naked and surrounded by a group of bearded beasts. There were plenty of onlookers from the neighboring windows. She stood silent, uncomprehending.

I stood there leaning against a steel monster—it seemed to be a tank. I began to bang my head against the steel.

When I opened my eyes it was very dark. Apparently from the beatings I lost an eye. Where I went, what I did, whether I walked or crawled, I do not know. Some villagers found me by a brook near Ilidza two days later and informed the Territorial Defense (Bosnian defense forces).

They are the only ones who visit me now. They call me "little sister" because of the pain we all share. Also because of our goal, Jihad. Misery makes us brothers and sisters.[82]

This story happens to be about Christians—people of my faith—hating, raping, and killing people because they are Muslims. But in the same area during the 1389 battle of Kosovo, it was Muslims hating and killings Orthodox Serbs, and the Serbs still have not forgotten. Nor have they forgotten when, during the Nazi-supported Croat regime, Roman Catholic priests forcibly baptized thousands of Orthodox Serbs living there. And now, how long will it be before little Jihad, if he still lives, forgets or forgives what happened to his grandmother, grandfather, and mother.

And this story has many other applications. Change the faith names to Hindu, Buddhist, Jew, indigenous peoples,...and this same story would apply in India, Sri Lanka, Ireland, Nigeria, Senegal, Iraq, Israel, Sudan, Algeria...What faith is now not involved in acts of hatred and violence in one or more of the 48 religious and ethnic wars now in progress?[83] What a revelation we have of the destructive hatred between followers of different faith traditions!

The second revelation comes from a meditation on Earth that has been continuing for about 1500 years, a meditation we usually call "science." From this meditation we know that Earth is the product of a 15-billion year journey from the first burst of creative energy. We know that we humans and all other life on Earth are intimately connected through a single, integral, and continuing creation journey and that we humans are related genetically to everything that contains the DNA molecule: to eagles, apes, snakes, frogs, trees, grasses, molds, bacteria...We are all distant cousins. And we all depend on each other through the complex bio-geo-chemical cycles of Earth. Earth is not just our home; we are Earth. Our entire physical being is made up of bits and pieces of Earth—water, air, rice, potatoes, etc.all of which are products of countless deaths. Life, at a point, concedes itself to death, and all new life has its origins in death. Collectively, we humans are an important part (but not the only part) of the consciousness of Earth.[84]

A third revelation derives in part from the second: we know now that the characterizations of man and woman, male and female, in the origin stories and traditions of many faiths are factually wrong and socially destructive. Sexual differentiation occurred very early in the continuing evolution and continuing creation of Earth, long before there was a human species, and the human female certainly has nothing to do with the origin or the perpetuation of a "dark side" of human nature. There is no defensible justification for any faith tradition perpetuating the pernicious falsehood that woman is the source of "evil" and "death" in human society. There is no justification for any man or for any male-dominated institution or faith defining man as superior to woman and normative for society.

The fourth revelation is that we humans have become co-creators of the future with the Divine. We humans—not as individuals, but as a species—will exercise an enormous influence on the future of Earth. Five billion of us individual humans, both poor and affluent, are acting today in ways that are destroying the life-sustaining capabilities of Earth and thereby destroying our own prospects. There is little question that we humans can destroy our species and many others with us. We can create an Earth future without humans. Now, nothing survives—no person, no species, no lake, no river, no ocean, no forest, no soil, no mountain, not even the atmosphere—unless we humans will it to survive. We can create a wasteland Earth-future or we can create a rich, vital Earth-future. We humans as a species will decide which way to go, for we have become co-creators with the Divine Earth-future.

This fourth revelation is of some considerable import, but to my knowledge, no faith tradition has prepared us for it. No faith anticipated the development of human power over Earth's future, this enormous responsibility. To my knowledge, no faith tradition has prepared us to know ourselves not as individuals but as a species. To my knowledge, no faith tradition has provided moral precepts to guide inter-species behavior, to decide which species should cease to exist, to understand which new species should be created through genetic engineering (and then patented), and to judge the alternative futures humans are considering for Earth.[85]

Where can we turn with questions about what to do, with questions that deal with matters of ultimate meaning and direction, with cherished beliefs, with fears and insecurities about the future? Where can we turn to learn to act responsibly as a species? Where can we turn for insights as to what possibilities there might be for a mutually enhancing human-Earth relationship in the future? Where can we turn for insights into what the original creative energy might desire our species—humans collectively—to make of Earth?

These are fundamentally spiritual questions, and they are being raised openly today in many communities, by scientists and economists, by philosophers and theologians, by historians and anthropologists, by religious and secular leaders alike.[86] Such questions are in the hearts of ordinary men and women who wonder about the future for all life and wonder how to answer their children's questions.

The questions being raised are unique to the experience and consciousness of peoples of our times, peoples who have looked into the farthest reaches of space, seen back in time to the very origins of the cosmos, have come to know Earth to be a relatively small planet in a galaxy of billions of stars and planets in a cosmos of billions of galaxies; people who have probed the core of the atom, lived with the prospect of nuclear annihilation, and now face the possibility of ecological annihilation. The questions are welling up from the human spirit struggling to be faithful to the moment, and a faith tradition, if it is to remain viable and relevant, must have answers to the ultimate questions welling up in the human spirit. So, in hope and trust, we turn to you, the carriers of our spiritual wisdom, with our questions.

What Shall We Do?

1. **What are the traditional teachings—and the range of other opinions—within your faith on how to meet the legitimate needs of the growing human community without destroying the ability of Earth to support the community of all life?**

    a. How does your faith tradition view the global trends that face us today? Does your faith tradition have people who monitor and understand global trends? How is information about global trends shared with the followers of your faith tradition?

    b. What does your faith tradition teach about how the needs of the poor and the wants of the rich are to be met as human numbers continue to grow? What trends and prospects do you see for the poor? What is the cause of poverty? Of greed?

    c. How are the needs and wants of humans to be weighed relative to the survival of other forms of life? What trends and prospects do you see for other forms of life? Does Earth exist for the human species to use in any way humans wish, independent of the welfare of other species? Is the human species justified in efforts to destroy species that limit the human food supply or the growth of human numbers?

d. What does your faith tradition teach concerning the proper relationship between the human species and all other species? Can the concepts of justice, unity, and peace be extended beyond the human community to the whole community of life?

e. What does your tradition teach about the taking of life? What does your tradition teach about humans killing humans? About humans killing members of other species—animals, plants? What teachings of your tradition might bear on the killing of *all* members of a species, the extinction of a species? What wisdom can you offer on the ethics of our species genetically modifying other species to create new races or even new species?

f. The origin stories of many faith traditions provide a basis for the human community valuing the whole community of life. Does your faith tradition have an origin story? If so, how does it place the human species relative to the whole community of life?

g. In addition to stories about the origin of life, there are stories about the continuation of life, about fertility. How do the fertility stories of your faith relate to its teachings on human procreation? How important are high fertility rates of the followers of your faith to the perpetuation of your tradition? How are its teachings to be understood today in light of the rapidly growing human population and the threat that even the present human population poses to the whole community of life? What norms are to be applied to the stewardship of the gift of human fertility? What cultural practices and technologies are appropriate for individuals to employ in regulating their own fertility?

h. There are also stories about abundance and fruitfulness of Earth and about human greed. What are human needs? When do needs become wants? How much is enough?

i. How are we to "value" the future in decisions we make today? What ethical and moral standards should be brought to "discounting" the interests of future generations in economic and other decisions made by us today? What does your faith tradition tell us about issues of intergenerational equity?

2. **What are the traditional teachings—and the range of other opinions—within your faith on the meaning of "progress" and how it is to be achieved?**

a. What dreams and hopes does your tradition inspire in young people?

b. What does your faith tradition offer as a vision for the future of Earth? For example, is the future of Earth viewed as a glorious climax, or a terrifying catastrophe, or something else entirely?

c. Is there some expectation in your tradition that humankind progresses through history toward some goal? If so, what is that understanding?

d. What does your faith tradition teach about the human destiny? Is the human destiny separable from that of Earth?

e. What is your destiny, the destiny of the followers of your faith tradition? What does your tradition teach concerning the destiny of followers of other traditions?

f. How are we to measure "progress?" Can there be progress for the human community without progress for the whole community of life?

g. How does your faith tradition relate personal "success" to "progress" for the whole? What is your image of a life well lived and how does that image relate to progress for the whole?

h. What does your faith tradition teach about human nature? What human qualities (sinfulness, fate, karma, freedom, greed, imagination, creativity) either limit or enhance what is possible for the individual or for society? What does your tradition teach with respect to fate, freedom of will, choice, and human responsibility? Is there a limit to how good humans can be? Or to how evil we can be?

i. How does your tradition respond to the suggestion that we humans are now capable of annihilating all life on Earth? Is the development of such a capability by humans anticipated in your faith tradition?

j. What is a "developed" country? What standards are to be applied in gauging the true state of development for a country? For example, is the United States a fully "developed" country? Is Haiti? Is India?

I, _____, do solemnly swear that I will support and defend the Constitution of the United States against all enemies, foreign and domestic; that I will bear true faith and allegiance to the same; and that I will obey the orders of the President of the United States and the orders of the officers appointed over me, according to the regulations and the Uniform Code of Military Justice. So help me God.

The enlistment oath,

United States military

forces

k. What does your tradition have to say about the scope of legitimate power of the nation-state? For example, is sovereignty a valid concept? Is any nation, institution, or group of people truly independent, subject to no other power on Earth?

l. What does your tradition teach about the ethics and morality of war? Under what circumstances are nations justified in going to war, declared or undeclared? How does your faith tradition value enmity versus solidarity?

m. When, if ever, is an individual entitled to kill for his or her country? When is an individual entitled to die for his or her country? When, if ever, is it appropriate to swear to kill upon order of an appointed officer? When is an individual, man or woman, entitled to design, manufacture, sell, or transport equipment for killing—weapons? What ethical and moral limitations, if any, does your tradition recognize on the types of weapons that individuals and nations may use to kill? How do the environmental consequences of war bear on the ethics and morality of using particular weapons or of warfare generally? What special moral considerations are associated with the use of "smart" weapons and other types of weapons that separate and distance the person using the weapon from the reality of his or her actions?

n. What teachings of your tradition bear on the establishment and control of the associations and corporations, which nation-states, under their laws, give the same legal status as people? What are the implications for faith and for society of creating such "fictitious persons" that are neither mortal nor concerned with ultimacy?

o. What does your faith tradition have to say about consumerism, about the manipulation and stimulation of desire, about advertising? Under what circumstances does one have enough?

3. **What are the traditional teachings—and the range of other opinions—within your faith tradition concerning a proper relationship with those who differ in race or gender (conditions one cannot change), or culture, politics, or faith?**

   a. Much hatred and violence is carried out in the name of religion. What teachings of your faith tradition have been used—correctly or not—in an attempt to justify such practices?

b. What can individuals or groups within your tradition do to reduce hatred and violence toward those who differ in race, gender, culture, politics, or faith?

c. What does your faith tradition teach—and practice—concerning the struggles of minorities (and even majorities) for freedom, both political and economic?

d. Discrimination and even violence by men toward women is often justified in the name of religion. Which, if any, of the teachings of your faith have been used—correctly or incorrectly—in this way?

e. Many faith traditions are singled out by women today as examples of "patriarchy." By "patriarchy," women refer to institutions or traditions that have defined man as superior to woman and normative for society. In your tradition, how long ago were the roles, rights, and responsibilities of men and women defined? What do your definitions imply about the superiority of men relative to women?

f. Are the current teachings of your tradition about the roles, rights, and responsibilities of women and men changing? If so, how? To what degree are women participating in the change process?

g. What does your faith tradition teach about the origin of truth and wisdom? For example, is your faith tradition the holder of the *only* divinely revealed truth?

h. How does your faith tradition characterize the teachings and followers of other faiths? Do some adherents of your tradition hold that the teachings and followers of other faiths are evil, dangerous, misguided? Is there any possibility that your faith tradition can derive wisdom, truth, or insight from the teachings of another faith?

i. Is it the responsibility of your faith tradition to bring your divinely revealed truth to the whole world? Are you to share your faith by example—by living it? Are you to ensure the future of your faith by producing children—more children than produced by the followers of other faiths? Are you to share your faith by teaching? By compelled conversion under threat of death, "ethnic cleansing," crusades, or war? Does your divine truth allow or encourage followers of your faith tradition to kill others who know a different divine truth?

4. **What are the traditional teachings—and the range of other opinions—within your faith on the possibility of criticism, correction, reinterpretation, and even rejection of ancient traditional assumptions and "truth" in light of new understandings or revelations?***

   a. Does your faith tradition envision new revelation, new understanding, new interpretation, new wisdom, and new truth concerning human activity affecting the future of Earth?*

   b. What are the most recent revelations in your faith concerning: the human community's relations with the whole community of life on Earth; the disparities of poverty and affluence within the human community; the human concept of progress; the superiority of men over women; and the use of violence toward those of a different faith, culture, race, or gender?

   c. How does your tradition respond to the revelation from the past 1,500 years of meditation on Earth and its origins—a revelation we usually call "science?" How will the disciplines of religious and scientific inquiry relate to each other in the future? Can science be a source of new inspiration for understanding and interpreting religious traditions? Can science provide new understanding of the primary, original source of religious insight—the universe itself?

---

* These questions—especially the inclusion of the word "revelation"—have caused concern and uneasiness among the followers and leaders of some faith traditions, and some have suggested an alternative question: "What are the teachings and resources within the tradition of your faith that may open up possibilities for new understanding, interpretation, and wisdom which would lead to a more developed religious teaching from an engagement with the data of science concerning human activity affecting the future of the earth?" The original wording expresses more clearly than the suggested rewording the question that I (and many others) have not only about my own faith (Christianity) but also about other faith traditions.[87]

CHANGING COURSE

In a sense, Earth is no longer orbiting peacefully about the Sun. Earth is careening toward the spiritual equivalent of a massive stone wall.

The brutality of humans to each other—the "ethnic cleansing," the ignoring of hunger and poverty, the acts of terrorism—and the environmental destruction and loss of natural beauty are already draining us of the spiritual and emotional energy we need to change course, and the situation is growing worse daily. We are becoming numb, unable to feel and react as we must if we are to put Earth back into a peaceful orbit.

Changing course will require an immense amount of energy. Not the energy that comes from coal, gas, oil, or even nuclear fuel, but rather spiritual and emotional energy, enough to change the thinking and lives of more than 5 billion people.

Can so much energy be generated? Can so many people become empowered to think and live differently? Maybe.

An Invitation to Help

It is the conviction of the Trustees and staff of the MILLENNIUM INSTITUTE that a unique opportunity to set Earth on a new course is offered by the 1999-2001 period, and we are working steadily to make the most of this opportunity. We invite spiritual leaders, and others, too, to join us in this effort.

The opportunity relates to the fact that deep in the human psyche is a compulsion to celebrate anniversaries, birthdays, and other recurring dates.[88] The entry into the 21st century and the third millennium will be a psychological experience vastly more profound than any anniversary we humans have yet experienced. Already hotel ballrooms are being booked along the Greenwich meridian by people who want to be the first to enter the 21st century. Concord supersonic jets are being chartered to fly people across time zones so that they can attend parties and celebrate the entry into the new millennium *twice*.[89] These are just the beginning signs of the emotional energies that will be released during the 1999-2001 period.[90]

This occasion, the entry into the new millennium, has special significance for Christians as the approximate bimillennium (2000th anniversary) of Christianity, and there is danger that it could come to be seen as an exclusively Christian event. The Gregorian calendar, however, never was an exclusively Christian calendar. Beginning the year at 1 January was a pagan Roman custom resisted by the Church, and most scholars now agree that the Nativity of Christ did not occur in 0 (or 1) A.D. but rather before Herod's death in 4 "B.C." Furthermore, the Gregorian calendar has become the calendar of commerce and science throughout the world.[91] The entry into the new millennium must be understood to be an anniversary of Earth to be enjoyed and celebrated by peoples of all faiths.

Earth's entry into the next millennium is a planetary "transitional" event,[92] and as a "mega anniversary" it has potential for reinforcing the identity of human beings, first and foremost, as citizens of Earth, as "Earthlings." This potential must be developed and utilized.

In most cultures, the transition from an old state to a new one (birthdays, graduations, marriages, funerals) is marked by celebrations having three elements. The first element is a period of preparation and grieving. During this period, we prepare to give up our past condition or to "die" to our old state. For our entry into the new millennium, we must prepare to give up our old, 20th century ways of thinking and living.

The second element is a moment of transition, the actual giving up of the old state and the entry into the new. It requires a symbolic act of change, such as the embrace or kiss at a wedding, the movement of the tassels at a graduation, the closing of the casket or the lighting of the pyre at a funeral. For our entry into the 21st century, we need a new symbol, perhaps crossing a stream or river to a new place and a new way of being.

The third element is the celebration of the new and its possibilities. Music, dance, song, and other forms of celebration are appropriate and needed. Gifts are an essential part of the celebration. Gifts are our way of expressing our good wishes and support for the new, and also a means of helping to ensure that something good and enduring comes of the new. For our entry into the new millennium, we must celebrate the opportunities and possibilities of the new era not only with music and joy, but also with generous gifts for the poor, for our enemies, and for Earth on this most extraordinary occasion.

Earth's entry into the next millennium cannot be just another major event. It cannot even be just the event of a lifetime. Or of a hundred years. Or even of a thousand years. That would not be enough. This must be *the* event of the whole Earth-time, the whole history of Earth. This must be the moment when humans interchange bad and good, unreal and real, and set themselves and Earth on a new course.

Over the next five years all 5 billion plus of us humans must prepare to die to 20th century ways of thinking and being. We must also prepare to see the possibilities and opportunities in our new condition in our new millennium.

To make these preparations, all 5 billion of us must devote the next five years to learning from each other about Earth and how to live sustainably and peacefully on Earth. Every person must learn to think in a way that leaves room in one's mind for the thoughts of others. Every person must come to understand much better how Earth's natural systems function and how human institutions, governments, political systems, social systems, international organizations, corporations, and spiritual institutions operate and influence the future of Earth. Every person must learn again the immense power and value of life. (Does all the money or wisdom in the whole world have the power to restore a single life?) Every person must learn to think like Earth, to act like Earth, to be Earth.

As a part of this learning process, we must all think through how our part of Earth can contribute to the new. Each person, each family, each corporate institution, each community, each country, each faith needs a plan to contribute to the new. What laws must be changed, what traditions, what beliefs, what institutions?

We also need ideas of appropriate gifts for Earth on this anniversary. What gift can a person give? What can a family, a corporate institution, a community, a country, a faith give to Earth on this momentous anniversary?

For this event to do what it must, the spiritual leaders of Earth must help lead the way and help plan the events. We humans, all five billion of us, depend on our spiritual leaders to make this all happen. Only the spiritual leaders of Earth—the recognized and the not-yet recognized—command the emotional energies needed to move heads of state, leaders of corporations and other institutions, and ordinary citizens to the acts of generosity and changed thinking and living that must occur.

We need you to lead us in teaching each other about Earth and how to live sustainably on Earth. We need you to help us all design a once-in-an-Earth-time celebration of Earth's entry into a new era. We need you to bring every person, every community, and every country to the celebration with their gifts. And most importantly, we need you to bring to the celebration a gift from your own faith tradition, a gift that will help change the course of Earth. What gift could your faith give Earth?

To do what must be done, Earth's spiritual leaders of all faiths and all traditions must work together in ways previously unimagined and unimaginable. We must count on you to develop a community of Earth's faith traditions that is an example of the kind of open communication, mutual respect, acceptance, cooperation, and good will that should characterize the emerging global community of nations and peoples. Each tradition has at its core a vision of Divine harmony that it urges its followers to embody in the social sphere. These visions have evolved in distinct historical and geographic contexts. The religions have not successfully been able to transcend their own historical origins so as to express their visions of unity in a fashion appropriate to the needs of the pluralistic global society that is taking form at the beginning of the new millennium.* The greatest single scandal in which Earth's faith traditions are now involved is their failure to practice their highest ethical ideals in their relations with one another.

As soon as we humans learn to think like Earth, we together will see a new future for Earth. Then we can die in peace, all 5 billion of us, to our old ways of thinking. We can cross the waters together. And we can celebrate Earth's safe arrival in a new era in a way that will be remembered forever.

---

* In his recent message acknowledging the Church's error in the conviction of Galileo, Pope John Paul II introduced some thoughts that might provide a basis not only for increased understanding and respect between science and religion, but also among religions. To paraphrase and abbreviate the Pope's argument:

The church must teach the truth, but what are we to do when a new scientific datum seems to contradict the truths of the faith?

There are two things we must do. First, it is a duty for theologians to keep themselves regularly informed of scientific advances in order to examine whether there are reasons for introducing changes in their teachings.

Second, it is necessary to recognize the distinction between Sacred Scripture and its interpretation. If it happens that authority of sacred Scripture is set in opposition to clear and certain reasoning, this must mean that the person who interprets scripture does not understand it correctly. Truth cannot contradict truth, and we may be sure that some mistake has been made.

Optimism, Hope, and Confidence

Many people, especially young people, look at our situation and prospects and ask, can we be optimistic? We have acted too slowly to help tens of millions of people, and if hundreds of millions, even billions, are to be spared the same fate, massive changes are needed over just the next few years. Can we be hopeful?

There is a difference between being optimistic and being hopeful. An optimistic person has a habitual disposition to expect the best possible outcome as the most likely. A hopeful person has a reasoned commitment to and faith in a good outcome, even though it may be unlikely in the light of past experience.

There is reason for us all to be hopeful but not optimistic. We can be hopeful because Earth is such a fertile, supporting place. We can be hopeful because Earth is showing remarkable resilience in the face of tremendous abuse. We can be hopeful because we now have a much greater understanding of Earth and its limits. We can be hopeful because we humans are recognizing that, as a species, we cannot indefinitely increase our numbers and our demands on Earth. We can be hopeful because we humans are beginning to recover from our erroneous notion that we are separate, above, and independent of all other life.

But perhaps something more than hope is justified. At least one person, Father Thomas Berry, thinks so:

> [W]e need to realize that the ultimate custody of the earth belongs to the earth. The issues we are considering are fundamentally earth issues that need to be dealt with in some direct manner by the earth itself. As humans

---

(...continued) From the Galileo affair we can learn a lesson that remains valid in relation to similar situations. In Galileo's time it was inconceivable to depict the world as lacking an absolute physical reference point, which could only be situated in the Earth or in the sun. Today, however, after Einstein and within the perspective of contemporary cosmology, neither of these two points of reference has the importance they once had. The lesson, therefore, is that often beyond two partial and contrasting perceptions there exists a wider perception that includes them and goes beyond both of them.

This lesson of Pope John Paul II might point the way for a new approach to the distrust, hatred, and violence that currently plagues interreligious relations. Might there be beyond the "partial and contrasting perceptions" of the many faith traditions "a wider perception that includes them and goes beyond...them?"[93]

we need to recognize the limitations in our capacity to deal with these comprehensive issues of the earth's functioning. So long as we are under the illusion that we know best what is good for the earth and for ourselves, then we will continue our present course, with its devastating consequences on the entire earth community.

Our best procedure might be to consider that we need not a human answer to an earth problem, but an earth answer to an earth problem. The earth will solve its problems, and possibly our own, if we will let the earth function in its own ways. We need only listen to what the earth is telling us.

Here we might observe that the basic mood of the future might well be one of confidence in the continuing revelation that takes place in and through the earth. If the dynamics of the universe from the beginning shaped the course of the heavens, lighted the sun, and formed the earth, if this same dynamism brought forth the continents and seas and atmosphere, if it awakened life in the primordial cell and then brought into being the unnumbered variety of living beings, and finally brought us into being and guided us safely through the turbulent centuries, there is reason to believe that this same guiding process is precisely what has awakened in us our present understanding of ourselves and our relation to this stupendous process...[94]

Let us all *listen to and allow ourselves to be guided* by the creative energy that shaped and lighted the universe from the beginning. Let us all awaken to a new understanding of ourselves and the continuing revelation that takes place in and through Earth. Let us *take back our lives* from cynicism, optimism, addictions, and despair. Let us *act* with conviction and confidence.

APPENDIX: WORLD PLANS FOR THE TURN OF THE MILLENNIUM

This appendix introduces the work of the Millennium Institute and surveys some of the efforts being made to use the turn of the millennium for lasting benefit of all peoples.

The Millennium Institute, a non-profit, charitable organization, grew out of *The Global 2000 Report to the President*, which I directed for President Jimmy Carter. After the publication of this 1980 analysis of foreseeable trends in the world's economy, population, resources, and environment, individual countries began asking for assistance with similar national studies. Since its founding in 1983, the Institute has supported such projects in 45 countries and developed a new tool for national budget formulation, the THRESHOLD 21 national sustainable development model.

By the Institute's tenth anniversary in 1993, our trustees could see progress toward sustainable development in many parts of world, but the pace seemed too slow to avoid some serious and unfortunate developments within the lifetime of people alive today. So we began thinking about using the millennial years 1999–2001 to accelerate the turn toward sustainability, an idea that fortunately has also occurred to many others.

What follows is a status report on world preparations for the year 2000. It begins with the Institute's 1993 proposal to spiritual leaders attending the Parliament of the World's Religions, reports the suggestions of people from around the word, and describes some of the current plans.

Further information on everything addressed in this Appendix can be found at the Web site maintained by the Millennium Institute: <http://www.igc.apc.org/millennium>.

Proposal to the Parliament

The Institute presented its millennium ideas first in an address I made to the 1993 Parliament of the World's Religions. Approximately 7,000 people from 200 faiths attended the nine-day meeting in Chicago. In my address, I summarized the interconnected challenges before humans at the turn of the millennium as described in this book, humanity's paralysis before the challenges, and the causes of our paralysis that are fundamentally spiritual in nature. I concluded with a request to the spiritual leaders of the world, the essence of which follows:

So I come to you our spiritual leaders with an overwhelming sense
that something is terribly wrong on Earth. I come to you with questions that are being raised openly today by parents and children, by
scientists and economists, by philosophers and theologians, by historians and anthropologists, by religious and secular leaders alike, as they
struggle to find their own sustainable faith and a new vision for the
future of Earth…

> *First,* how are we to meet the legitimate needs of the growing
> human community without destroying the ability of Earth to
> support the community of all life?

> *Second,* what is the meaning of "progress" and how is it to be
> achieved? Can there be progress for the human species at the
> expense of the whole community of life?

> *Third,* how should we relate to those who differ in race or gen-
> der, or culture, or politics, or especially faith? How can inter-
> religious hatred and violence be eliminated?

> *Fourth,* how should my faith tradition—and yours—allow for
> criticism, correction, reinterpretation, and even rejection of
> ancient traditional assumptions? How are we to incorporate
> new understandings or revelations, especially the new scientific
> truths with spiritual significance.

Are you, our spiritual leaders, prepared to grapple honestly with these
questions? Are you willing to engage in open and sincere dialogue with
scientists who are bringing us truths never known before in human history? Are you willing to admit the possibility of need for reinterpretation
and even rejection of ancient traditions and assumptions? If you are,
then perhaps together we humans can dream a new dream, which is
our only possible answer [the challenges ahead].

But to dream is not enough. We must also act, and to act we must be
inspired. We humans need an occasion that inspires us and brings
out in us our very best instincts —like a 50th wedding anniversary or
a 100th birthday does…

We have such an occasion approaching. The occasion is the year 2000,
and I would like to tell you a dream I have for the year 2000…

Earth's entry into the next millennium cannot be just a major event. It
cannot even be just the event of a lifetime. Or even the event of a

thousand years. That would not be nearly enough. Earth's entry into the millennium must be the time when humans begin to live peacefully, justly, and sustainably on Earth. If it is, the turn of the millennium will be the event of all time. And if it isn't, it will be nothing.

Now, I have a request, to you, our spiritual leaders—a request that I make on behalf of, not just all humans, but on behalf of the whole community of life. Would you devote the next 7 years of your lives to helping all 6 billion of us humans to learn from each other and from Earth how to live peacefully, justly, and sustainably on the Earth in the next millennium? Would you help us all—*would you help Earth*—dream a new dream?

Would you put away hatred and work together in ways previously unimagined and unimaginable? Would you develop a community of earth's faith traditions that is an example of the kind of open communication, mutual respect, acceptance, cooperation, and good will that should characterize the emerging global community of nations and peoples?

Would you lead the way to a planet-wide spiritual celebration of Earth's entry into a new era?

Would you bring every person, every community, and every country to the celebration with appropriate gifts? And most importantly, would you and your faith tradition come too, bringing a gift that will change the course of Earth?

If you will, the original source of creative energy will show us all a new future.

Then, with hope in our hearts, we can die in peace—*all 6 billion of us*—die to our old, immature, 20th-century ways of being and thinking. We can cross the waters together. And we can *celebrate Earth's arrival in a new era* in a way that will be remembered forever.

Suggestions from Roundtable Meetings, Scholars, and Organizers

The proposal was well received and opened the way for many discussions of the idea of using the turn of the millennium to promote a peaceful, just, and sustainable future.

Since the 1993 Parliament, the Institute convened or participated in "millennium roundtable" meetings in Addis Ababa, Amsterdam, Beijing, Berlin, Cape Town, Chicago, Dallas, Dhaka, the Hague, Islamabad, Istanbul, Jeddah, Lilongwe, London, New Delhi, New York, Ottawa, Paris, Reykjavik, Rio de Janeiro, Rome, Tokyo, San Francisco, San Jose, and Washington. We have also consulted millennium scholars and organizers, including Dr. Hillel Schwartz, author of *Century's End,* and Mr. Peter Aykroyd, author of *The Anniversary Compulsion.* From these meetings and consultations, a few core concepts emerged:

1. For the turn of the millennium to have universal significance, it must belong to and have participation of all peoples and all faiths.

2. For the turn of the millennium to alter anything as fundamental as the human future, it must inspire a new dream, a new vision of human future, of "progress."

3. A viable dream for the future must embrace peace, justice, and sustainability: Peace, because the alternative is unjust and unsustainable. Justice for its own right, and because injustice is the cause of so many wars. Sustainability, because everything depends ultimately on the life systems of Earth sustaining us.

4. For the turn of the millennium to produce change at the level needed, it needs to be a unique rite of passage, a time when, together, 6,000 million people "die" to an old era of existence and enter the next as a new, changed person.

5. For the turn of the millennium to produce significant change, it must involve both personal change of large numbers of people and the realignment of many large institutions, which act in society as very powerful "fictitious persons."

6. Through "Millennium Gifts"—what we choose to leave behind in the 20th century and what to take across to the 21st—there is an opportunity for each of us individually, all 6,000 million of us, and each organization and institution to participate in shaping the new era.

7. Goals for the turn of the millennium must be relatively modest—a new vision of where we want to go, a resetting of the rudder, and an expanding group committed to continuing the

work—because the task of creating a peaceful, just, and sustainable future is the most difficult task humans have ever undertaken and it will require at least a century of dedicated effort.

8. Thousands of useful millennium activities are planned, and the chances of their capturing world attention and inspiring large, lasting change will be increased by sharing and cooperating.

The Institute is following these suggestions with its program.

Millennium Gifts

In many cultures people give enduring gifts at birth and at life's turning points. The turn of the millennium is a turning point in the life of everyone.

Millennium Gifts contribute to a sustainable future in one or more of the following ways:

1. promoting social justice and economic equity,

2. preventing or curtailing pollution,

3. maintaining ecosystems, protecting the diversity of life, and slowing human population growth,

4. conserving energy and natural resources while respecting Earth's natural cycles, or

5. promoting the nonviolent resolution of conflicts.

Each Millennium Gift is something we carry across the threshold of a new millennium on behalf of a sustainable world. A Millennium Gift can be given by an individual, a community, a corporation, a profession, a faith, a government, or any other group or organization.

Groups working toward a sustainable future benefit from a Millennium Gift program, and several of those listed below have established such programs. We invite you to shape the future by giving a gift. There are no costs or requirements; just do it. Then tell us about it. We want 2000 significant gifts by 2000. Gifts will be listed on the Millennium Institute Web site and publicized at special turn of the millennium events.

A Sharing and Cooperating Web Site: <http://www.igc.apc.org/millennium>

The Millennium Institute maintains a web site to encourage sharing and cooperating on millennium events and programs. The site covers State of Our World Indicators, Millennium Threshold Events country by country, design tips for Turn of the Millennium Events, The Institute's THRESHOLD 21 national sustainable development model, links to other useful sites, and opportunities to subscribe to newsletters.

Key International Events and Activities

The turn of the millennium is inspiring a huge number of events, meetings, fairs, programs, publications, and so on. Most have the character of a celebration at "milepost 2000" and a "looking back" at our accomplishments at reaching here. Some have a "looking ahead" aspect. The selected list that follows focuses on those that look ahead and are international in scope. Additional information can be found on the Institute's Web page.

> *Abolition 2000,* a citizens' movement for an international treaty to eliminate nuclear weapons on a specific schedule, to be signed by 2000.

> *Catalyst,* an international gathering of 30,000 to 50,000 young people to envision and carry out community-based actions to create the 21st century that young people desire for their future.

> *Demilitarization for Democracy/Year 2000 Campaign,* an effort to achieve a large-scale, mutually agreed reduction in military forces and spending by 2000 under UN administration, and to redirect savings into human development.

> *Earth Charter,* a statement of fundamental principles of a global partnership for sustainable development and environmental conservation to be adopted by the UN Millennium General Assembly in 2000.

> *Earth Day 2000,* an international campaign for huge meetings and events around the world on Earth Day, April 22, 2000, and for media attention to the issues of sustainable development leading up to Earth Day 2000.

Expo 2000, a world's fair in Hannover, Germany, celebrating the human arrival at 2000 and looking ahead at the challenges of the 21st century. Building designs and displayed technologies are imaginative ways of addressing some of the challenges of the future.

Forum 2000, a series of Presidential conferences on the issues of and visions for the 21st century sponsored by the government of the Czech Republic.

Foundation for the Progress of Humanity, a source of inspiration and funding for an international network of non-governmental organizations envisioning and planning a desirable 21st century.

Global Action Plan, a civil society effort to reduce waste and pollution household-by-household in communities throughout the industrial world through service contracts with local and state government agencies.

Global Meeting of Generations, a series of international, intergenerational dialogues about the future organized by a 12-member coalition.

International Peace Conference, an effort by the Hague Appeal for Peace to leave war behind in the 20th century by de-legitimizing war now.

IUCN Commission on Environmental Law, a hard law treaty to achieve the principles of the Earth Charter, to be submitted to the UN Millennium General Assembly.

Jubilee 2000, a worldwide campaign to cancel the crushing international debt of impoverished countries—a wonderful Millennium Gift—by the new millennium, and provide a debt-free start to a billion people worldwide.

Millennium Children's Conference, 1,000 youth leaders meeting for five days in five international sites to review lessons from the past millennium and set priorities for the next.

Millennium General Assembly, a UN general assembly meeting called by the Secretary General for the year 2000.

Millennium Project, an analysis of issues, opportunities, and strategies for the future by an international group of futurists.

National Geographic Society Millennium Project, a series of articles to introduce the key issues of the coming years to the world community.

National Millennium Commissions, an organizational approach pioneered by France, Italy, the United Kingdom, and the United States. Many governments are now forming millennium councils or commissions. The United States and Italy are cohosting a first meeting of millennium commissions in Rome in June 1998.

Parliament of the World's Religions, a December 1999 gathering of world spiritual leaders in Cape Town, South Africa. Building on its 1993 Declaration of a Global Ethic, the parliament will support the creation of a peaceful, just, and sustainable future through a Call for Change addressed to the world's guiding institutions: religion, government, business, media, science, and education. Through its Projects 2000, the Parliament will also call on people of every faith to make Millennium Gifts.

Pole to Pole 2000, an international team of young people trekking from the North Pole to the South Pole during the year 1999 distributing information on sustainability issues en route and calling for Millennium Gifts.

Smithsonian Institution Millennium Program, a series of conferences, events, and exhibits on sustainable development in the new millennium.

State of the World Forum, international forums and media events in 1998, 1999, and 2000 on "Our Common Enterprise," which in essence is to create a peaceful, just, and sustainable future.

Sydney 2000 Olympic Games, one in continuing series of Olympic Games, but with some additional attention to energy and water conservation, waste avoidance, pollution management, and protection of the natural and cultural environment.

Talk 2000 and Let's Talk 2000, an international Internet conference and monthly e-mail bulletin (<talk2000@rmii.net.com>) discussing the folklore, festivities and impact of the millennial years 1999–2001 on the future of civilization.

The Great Millennium Peace Ride, a youth bicycle ride around the world in 2000 promoting peace and sustainability.

The Natural Step, a global program encouraging corporations to adopt sustainable practices for the new millennium.

The People's Assembly, a meeting of non-governmental organizations to be held in parallel with the UN Millennium General Assembly.

The Tidewater Summit, an annual meeting of heads of development banks and development agencies. For the first time in 30 years, part of the 1998 meeting will be public with a millennial (looking back, looking forward) examination of development issues. Since millennial "looking ahead" agenda is the same as the global development agenda, the Tidewater Meeting will set a tone for many other millennium meetings.

Twenty First Century Initiative, an effort, using TV programming, Internet, and print media, to build awareness by 2000 of the enormous changes happening to our world and their causes, and to spur innovation.

UNICEF, achieving by 2000 the goals of the World Summit for Children.

United Religions Initiative, an effort to envision a way to bring world's religions together under a common charter by 2000 and to call for a global cease-fire.

World Muslim Congress, an international program in 68 countries to involve Muslims in millennium gifts programs, research issues for the future, and in the 1999 Parliament of the World's Religions.

World Wildlife Fund, Living Planet Campaign, an effort to create a living legacy for ourselves and our children through Millennium Gifts preserving the world's most outstanding habitats, and the plants and animals they contain.

Each of these groups is doing work that is changing the world. They need your support and encouragement. Further information on each is available on the Millennium Institute's Web site.

We know this list is incomplete. Please send us information on others that should be included. Our e-mail address is: <millennium@igc.apc.org>. We will continue to add to the list of organizations on the Millennium Institute Web site.

A New Vision

Implicit in the activities, events, and projects listed above is a craving for a new vision, a new direction, a new concept of "progress." Over the past few decades, many reports and books from around the world have also expressed aspects of a new vision or desired direction. The Institute has collected dozens of such reports and is in the process of digesting them and synthesizing the vision elements they contain. A preliminary draft will be available by the end of 1998. We hope then to invite suggestions and contributions from many others, especially those working on millennium events and projects such as those just listed.

The Thingvellir Meeting

In a 1991 letter to the Government of Iceland and in the 1993 address to the Parliament of the World's Religions, the Institute proposed a global transitional event to mark the turn of the millennium.

The original idea was a summit meeting of spiritual leaders and heads of state at Thingvellir National Park in Iceland. Thingvellir is a natural amphitheater seating 30,000 in a beautiful valley through which a clean, blue river flows. It was formed by separation of the European and American plates, and thus holds East and West together. The rift stretches from the North Pole to the South, thus linking the Northern and Southern hemispheres. But most importantly, Thingvellir is by Icelandic tradition a place where even enemies meet and talk, and no weapon has been at this place since it was set aside as a special meeting place in the year 930 by the Icelandic Parliament, the oldest continuing parliament in the world. What better place could there be for a meeting to mark the human departure from one era and entry into another?

The proposal generated much interest in Iceland and has been discussed at all levels of government, in the media, and at a special international conference. While Icelandic leaders recognize the merits of the meeting, they doubt that heads of state would take the event seriously. Furthermore, conversations with many people around the world suggest that heads of state, on average, are not regarded as carriers of the values needed for a peaceful, just, and sustainable future. A smaller meeting at Thingvellir focused on developing a vision and plan for the future and a new kind of alliance committed to long-term work is still under consideration.

A Final Word

The world is at a turning point. A continuation along the course set by the trends of the 20th century does not lead to a peaceful, just, and sustainable future. There are alternative courses that are better for everyone, and now—at the turn of the millennium—is the time to reset our course.

Gerald O. Barney
Executive Director
MILLENNIUM INSTITUTE

APPENDIX: Bangladesh's Children at Threshold 21— Investment in Desirable Futures

As we approach the millennial turn, it has become clear, more than ever before, that a far-reaching and deep-rooted social transformation needs to take place. H.G. Wells once observed that history looks more and more like a "race between education and catastrophe." This is definitely true for the world as a whole, as Dr. Gerald O. Barney, Jane Blewett, and Kristen R. Barney show in their analysis of world trends and alternative futures in this book. And around the world it is nowhere more true than in Bangladesh today.

In fact, the choices described in this book as facing the world in the future are the same ones facing Bangladesh today. Becoming a learning society and using available means and technologies will be the only way for Bangladesh to turn her population from liability to asset, to counter the persistent, draining, and disabling multiple poverties that hold back growth, deny opportunity, and perpetuate suffering and inequity. By using powerful modeling tools such as THRESHOLD 21,* developed by the Millennium Institute, and by reading this book we will get a better view of not only what are currently our probable futures, but also what can be our possible futures. These provide us with both the compelling evidence and the critical path we need to take to change and to transform ourselves and our global society.

THRESHOLD 21 also shows the urgency with which we need to act. In the next 35 years, Bangladesh's population will just about double—some

---

* THRESHOLD 21 is a computer-based national sustainable development model that assesses in an integrated manner the impacts on development of policy decisions in education, demographics, health care, HIV/AIDS, nutrition, agriculture, industry, services, trade, energy, water, forests, pollution and technology. Assessments are made in term of many indicators, including National Accounts, World Bank's National Wealth Indicators, and UN indicators (Development Assistance Framework, World Summit for Children, Human Development Index, Gender Development Index, and UNCSD Sustainable Development Indicators). The THRESHOLD 21 model can be tailored to sub-national levels to analyze a region, a sector, or a specific policy, or a group of nations together. The model enables the user to trace each impact back to its root causes. THRESHOLD 21 is the result of 20 years of research on national models. It became operational in early 1994, and was first placed in use in Bangladesh, the most populous LLDC, under the sponsorship of United Nations agencies, including UNICEF.

200 million people crowded into a poor, small, and fragile country. If that future nation were merely today's on a larger scale, then 140 million people, mostly children, would be undernourished; 50,000 women would die each year from causes related to pregnancy; and 1 million children would die before their first birthday. There would be at least 18 million child laborers, 88 million illiterate adults, and 1,500 people per square kilometer, exerting unprecedented ecological pressure. This would be accompanied by rising landlessness and joblessness, a flight to cities with niggardly infrastructures, and an increasingly desperate struggle for survival that could produce massive social dislocation leading even to national upheaval.

Indeed, many of the world's persistent development challenges find their more extreme expression in Bangladesh: overpopulation, underdevelopment, natural disasters, malnutrition, gender discrimination, illiteracy, morbidity, and premature mortality. There have also been poverties of tolerance, confidence, and a belief that things can and must change—both within as well as outside the country.

But these dismal projections and predicaments need not be. There is nothing inevitable about them. They largely reflect unconscious but pervasive preferences from the past, and outmoded but persistent priorities of privilege in the present. In fact, there are really no mysteries in how to bend those projections or how to overcome these predicaments.

With resilience and innovation, Bangladesh already has come to shatter several development myths and conventional wisdoms. It has been a pioneer of a new paradigm in which relatively small but strategic investments are having payoffs far beyond the spreadsheet. Poor, disenfranchised women are gaining confidence and participation in society in addition to having been proved eminently bankable. Primary school dropouts and leftouts eagerly learn from para-teachers in makeshift schools. Private-sector salt manufacturers contribute to people's intelligence by iodizing their salt. Reductions in fertility and infant morality are taking a fraction of the time they took in Europe or the United States. Child laborers from the garment industry are put in nongovernmental organization (NGO) schools with financial help from the private sector. Massive social mobilization for immunization has virtually eradicated polio.

Most of these achievements as well as the conclusions derived from THRESHOLD 21 point to a compelling and overarching truth: children are central to sustainable development and to human progress. Working through the child of today is the most effective way to create a healthy, intelligent, productive, and peaceful population 25 years from now. It cannot be done faster. And any other way will simply not be as effective. For human and societal development to accelerate and to deepen, we must begin with the child. The most critical times and phases occur early in life, when certain things *must* happen, when certain minima must be met—or else irreversible damage will be inflicted, irretrievable loss incurred. So, precisely because we are concerned with the longer run of societal evolution, we must invest ourselves and our resources in the short run in the child.

UNICEF's mandate is to work in alliance with countries and communities to meet specific end-decade goals for children, to fulfill and to protect the rights of children and women. The responses to these challenges and opportunities are inextricably linked with macro processes including population dynamics, environmental changes, economic adjustments, international trade and policy implementation, and the realization of commitments to social-sector investment priorities. In Bangladesh, innovative programmatic building blocks have been evolved by UNICEF and our partners to meet the basic needs and to fulfill the rights of children and women, laying the foundation for a new paradigm and future. These include:

1. A teaching and learning approach based on the multiple intelligences theory is boosting attendance rates, learning achievements, ownership on the part of teachers and communities of school management, as well as color, life, and joyful laughter in primary school classrooms.

2. Learning opportunities for working children, particularly those in hazardous and exploitative occupations, are being created. In the garment industry, a model for co-operative action among industry, U.N. agencies, government, and NGOs was evolved and implemented in the best interests of the child in a "win-win-win" formula, whereby the children, the country and the industry all benefited.

3. An initiative to control childhood malnutrition is bringing together cost-effective, sustainable, community-based interventions with improvement of caring practices and monitoring systems, while strengthening management and participation by local governments and community members, particularly women.

4. An approach to reducing maternal mortality uses the health system as an entry point for launching activities aimed at enhancing
women's status and addressing violence against women through
an initiative to render "women-friendly" services and bring about
change in attitudes and practices.

5. A "Facts for Life" communication initiative is providing families
and providers of care to children with the practical knowledge
they need to maximize their children's physical and psychological potential and development from the very start of life.

6. A low-cost method of overcoming post-traumatic stress disorders
is promising to address and alleviate the significant economic
implications of trauma, which perpetuate a vicious cycle of suffering, deprivation and lost opportunities among battered
women, abused children, victims of natural disasters, refugees,
and traumatized war veterans.

7. A new global cosmology for our children, put into curricular format, is based on dramatic new insights from the frontiers of science, inviting us to reflect on who we really are in this universe,
whose origin, development, and destiny beckons us to look
deeper into ourselves as we look farther into the past and into
the future.

8. All this requires new ways of meeting, decision-making, and conflict resolution that bring together stakeholders and key actors on
priority issues. The Future Search Conference methodology has
been effectively used in Bangladesh, leading to meetings where
attention is paid not only to the subject matter but also to the
psycho-social dynamic—meetings where all the stakeholders on
an issue are given all the opportunities they need to express what
they need, in a safe place in which fear, guilt, ignorance, anger,
pride, and sorrow are all acknowledged. Participants have iden-
tified risks and opportunities, and have interwoven contributions
and made concrete commitments in areas including early childhood education, countering HIV/AIDS, eliminating iodine defi-
ciencies, and preventing deaths from diarrhea.

Although the impact that the above will have on the macro outlook of
society may not be apparent at first, picture the following: just as the
graphs in THRESHOLD 21 show what a child born today can expect to happen

during her lifetime, the above enable us to project realistically into the future a Bangladesh with a healthy, productive population, educated not only in how to read and write, but also with the skills and capacity to solve problems, resolve conflicts, and give the best care possible equally to future generations of girls and boys, all with the understanding that this is a strategy of socioeconomic practicality as well a matter of right.

THRESHOLD 21 will thus be very valuable in UNICEF's advocacy and planning activities, for, as a powerful integrated tool that weighs the relative merits of making investments in different types of development projects in the long term, it enables us to look at children's issues as part of a whole system and better understand their role and the power of their potential. This is a valuable contribution to global co-operation and partnership, since it shows organizations and policymakers which are the most strategic actions to take. And for Bangladesh, we simply cannot afford not to be on the critical path to accelerate the demographic transition toward population stability.

On behalf of UNICEF, I would also like to thank the many NGOs and research organizations, including the Millennium Institute, with which we worked to develop THRESHOLD 21 to help guide Bangladesh's sustainable development efforts. Part of the reason why UNICEF invested in the design of THRESHOLD 21 was the expectation that the model would be used by key Bangladeshi institutions, such as The Bangladesh Institute of Development Studies and the Planning Commission, which would periodically generate perspectives with strategic assessments for the short, medium, and long term.

It is through these integrated approaches and enhanced vision that Bangladesh will respond to her challenges. Bangladesh is a microcosm of the developing world, and her achievements in social development epitomize what great things can be achieved even under adverse conditions. Bangladesh is at once a challenge to herself and a giant cause for optimism. Believing is seeing. And I believe that we can still achieve the survival and developmental goals for the year 2000, that meeting the most basic needs of the world's children could be our gift to all of humanity at the millennial turn.

Rolf C. Carriere
Representative
UNICEF Bangladesh

REFERENCES

[1] Barney, G. O. 1980. *The Global 2000 Report to the President*, Volumes 1, 2, and 3. Washington: U.S. Government Printing Office.

[2] Nasseef, Dr. Abdullah Omar. 1995. Personal communication.

[3] Nováček, P. 1992. Personal communication.

[4] Pimental, D. 1992. *Competition for Land: Development, Food, and Fuel.* In Kuliasha, M. A.; Zucher, A.; and Ballew, K. J., Eds. *Technologies for a Greenhouse Constrained Society.* Boca Raton: Louis Publishers. 1992. pp. 325-348.

[5] U.S. Department of Agriculture, Economic Research Service, Commodity Economics Division, Trade Analysis Branch. 1993. Based on Agrostate data from the U.N. Food and Agriculture Organization, Rome.

[6] For a well-written description of what happens when there is not enough food to feed a large number of people, see: Brown, D. 1993. "Starving Somalis Face Ultimate Survival Test: As Malnutrition Leaches Cells' Needs, the Human Body Rations Remaining Glucose." *The Washington Post.* 4 January 1993. p. A1.

[7] United Nations. 1992. *Long-Range World Population Projections.* New York: United Nations. p. 22.

[8] United Nations. 1992. *Ibid.*

[9] Kristof, N. D. 1993. "China's Crackdown on Births: A Stunning, and Harsh, Success." *The New York Times.* 25 April 1993. p. A1.

[10] Ruttan, V. W. 1990. "Constraints on Sustainable Growth in Agricultural Production: Into the 21st Century." In: Agriculture and Rural Development Department and Training Division, World Bank, eds. 1991. *Eleventh Agricultural Symposium: Agricultural Issues in the Nineties.* Washington: The World Bank.

[11] U.N. Food and Agriculture Organization. 1989. FAO Production Yearbook tapes. Rome: U.N. Food and Agriculture Organization.

[12] Ruttan, V. W. December 1992. Personal communication.

[13] Ruttan, V. W. 1990. "Constraints on Sustainable Growth in Agricultural Production: Into the 21st Century." In: Agriculture and Rural Development Department and Training Division, World Bank, eds. 1991. *Eleventh Agricultural Symposium: Agricultural Issues in the Nineties.* Washington: The World Bank.

[14] Brown, L. R. 1970. *Seeds of Change: The Green Revolution and Development and the 1970s.* New York: Praeger Publishers. Dalrymple, D. 1980. *Development and Spread of Semi-Dwarf Wheat and Rice in the United States: An International Perspective.* Washington: U.S. Department of Agriculture. Crosby, A. W., Jr. 1972. *The Columbian Exchange: The Biological and Cultural Consequences of 1492.* Westport, CT: Greenwood Press. Viola, H. J. and Margolis, C. 1991. *Seeds of Change.* Washington: The Smithsonian Institution Press.

[15] Carroll, C. R.; Vandermeer, J. H.; and Rosset, P. M. 1990. *Agroecology.* New York: McGraw-Hill Publishing Company, 641 pages.

[16] National Research Council. 1989. *Alternative Agriculture.* Washington: National Academy Press. 448 pages.

[17] Ruttan, V. W., ed. 1993. *Agriculture, Environment, and Health: Toward Sustainable Development into the 21st Century.* Minneapolis: University of Minnesota Press. Ruttan, V. W. 1990. "Constraints on Sustainable Growth in Agricultural Production: Into the 21st Century." In: Agriculture and Rural Development Department and Training Division, World Bank, eds. 1991. *Eleventh Agricultural Symposium: Agricultural Issues in the Nineties.* Washington: The World Bank. Ruttan, V. W. December 1992. Personal communication.

[18] Leopold, A. 1953. *Round River.* New York: Oxford University Press.

[19] Masters, C. D., et al. 1991. *Ibid.*

[20] Raven, P. H. 1987. *We're Killing Our World: The Global Ecosystem in Crisis.* Occasional Paper. Chicago: The MacArthur Foundation. pp. 12- 13.

[21] Wilson, E. O. 1993. "Is Humanity Suicidal?" *The New York Times Magazine.* 30 May 1993. p. 24.

[22] Ruttan, V. W. December 1992. Personal communication.

[23] Hubbert, M. K. 1977. "World Oil and Natural Gas Reserves and Resources." In: Congressional Research Service. *Project Independence: U.S. and World Energy Outlook Through 1990.* Washington: Government Printing Office. pp. 632-644. Neehring, R. 1978. *Giant Oil Fields and World Oil Resources.* Santa Monica, CA: Rand Corp. Masters, C.D.; Root, D. H.; and Attanasi, E. D. 1991. "Resource Constraints in Petroleum Production Potential." *Science.* 12 July 1991, vol. 253, pp. 146-152.

[24] Masters, C. D.; Root, D. H.; and Attanasi, E. D. 1991. "Resource Constraints in Petroleum Production Potential." *Science.* 12 July 1991, vol. 253. pp. 146-152.

[25] Masters, C. D.; et al. 1991. *Ibid.*

[26] Pimental, D. and Dazhong, W. "Technological Changes in Energy Use in U.S. Agricultural Production." In: Carol, C. R.; Vandermeer, J. H.; and Rosset, P. M. *Agroecology.* New York: McGraw Hill Publishers. 1990. p. 154.

[27] Energy Information Administration. 1992. *Annual Energy Outlook 1992.* Washington: U.S. Department of Energy. DOE/EIA-3083 (92). p. 6; and Oak Ridge National Laboratory. 1989. *Energy and Technology R&D—What Could Make a Difference?* as reported in: U.S. Department of Energy. 1991. *National Energy Strategy.* Washington: U.S. Government Printing Office.

[28] Goldberg, J., et al. 1985. "Basic Needs and Much More One Kilowatt Per Capita." *Ambio.* vol. 14, no. 4-5, pp. 190-200. Levins, A. B. 1977. *Soft Energy Paths: Toward a Durable Peace.* Cambridge, MA: Bellinger.

[29] Reuters. 1993. "SDI, Chernobyl Helped End Cold War, Conference Told." *New York Times.* 27 February 1993. p. A17.

[30] See, for example: Daly, H. E. and Cobb, J. B., Jr. 1989. *For the Common Good: Redirecting the Economy Toward Community and the Environment and a Sustainable Future.* Boston: Beacon Press; and Ahmad, Y. J.; El Serafy, S.; Lutz, E. 1989. *Environmental Accounting for Sustainable Development.* Washington: The World Bank.

[31] Daly, H. E. and Cobb, J. B., Jr. 1989. *For the Common Good: Redirecting the Economy Toward Community and the Environment and a Sustainable Future.* Boston: Beacon Press.

[32] Turner, B. L., II, et al. 1990. *The Earth As Transformed by Human Action.* New York: Cambridge University Press.

[33] UNEP/GEMS. 1987. *The Greenhouse Gases.* Nairobi: United Nations Environment Programme.

[34] Intergovernmental Panel on Climate Change. 1992. *1992 IPCC Supplement.* Geneva: World Meteorological Organization. p. 25. New historical data show that massive changes in the average global temperature can occur in decades rather than in centuries. Sullivan, W. "Study of Greenland Ice Finds Rapid Change in Past Climate." *The New York Times.* July 1993. p. A1.

[35] Watson, R. T. and Albritton, D. C. 1991. *Scientific Assessment of Ozone Depletion: 1991.* Geneva: World Meteorological Organization. p. ES-v.

[36] Intergovernmental Panel on Climate Change. 1990. *Policymakers Summary of the Scientific Assessment of Climate Change.* Geneva: World Meteorological Organization. pp. 22-23.

[37] Intergovernmental Panel on Climate Change. 1990. *Policymakers Summary of the Scientific Assessment of Climate Change.* Geneva: World Meteorological Organization. p. 33.

[38] Global Environment Monitoring System. 1987. *The Greenhouse Gases.* Nairobi: U.N. Environment Programme.

[39] Watson, R. T. and Albritton, D. C. 1991. *Scientific Assessment of Ozone Depletion: 1991.* Geneva: World Meteorological Organization. p. ES-v.

[40] UNEP/GEMS. 1987. "The Ozone Layer," Nairobi: United Nations Environment Programme.

[41] Stevens, W. K. "Peril to Ozone Hastens a Ban on Chemicals." *The New York Times.* 26 November 1992. p. A1.

[42] Watson, R. T. and Albritton, D. C. 1991. *Scientific Assessment of Ozone Depletion: 1991.* Geneva: World Meteorological Organization. ES-i - ES-viii. Gleason, J. F., et al. 1993. "Record Low Global Ozone in 1992." Science. vol. 260. 23 April 1993. pp. 523-526. Kerr, R. A. 1993. "Ozone Takes a Nose Dive After The Eruption of Mt. Pinatubo." Science. vol. 260. pp. 490-491.

43 Gen. 13:1-12

44 For details on Zaïre , see Nobel, K. B. 1992. "As the Nation's Economy Collapses, Zaïrians Squirm Under Mobutu's Heel." *The New York Times.* 30 August 1992. p. 14. "Zaïre Farce." 1992. *The Economist.* 12 December 1992. pp. 53-4. Wa Mutua, M. "The Last Chapter?" *Africa Report.* September/October 1992. pp. 54-56. Linden, E. "Kinshasa, Zaïre ." *Time.* 11 January 1993. pp. 30-31. Lumumba-Kasongo, T. "Zaïre's Ties to Belgium: Persistence and Future Prospects in Political Economy." *Africa Today.* 3rd Quarter 1992. pp. 23-48.

45 Turnbull, C. M. 1972. *The Mountain People.* New York: Simon and Schuster. pp. 131-132.

46 Kamm, H. 1993. "'People Smugglers' Send New Tide of Refugees Onto Nordic Shores." *The New York Times.* 15 February 1993. p. A1.

47 Kamm, H. "In Europe's Upheaval, Doors Close to Foreigners." *The New York Times.* 10 February 1993. p. A1.

48 Simmons, M. "The Sex Market: Scourge on the World's Children." *The New York Times.* 9 April 1993. p. A3.

49 Bread for the World. 1990. *Hunger 1990: A Report on the State of World Hunger.* Washington: Bread for the World Institute on Hunger and Development.

50 Buber, M. 1958. *I and Thou.* New York: Collier Books.

51 Nhât Hanh, T. 1988. *The Heart of Understanding: Commentaries on the Prajnaparamita Heart Sutra.* Berkeley, CA: Parallax Press. pp. 33-38.

52 For other examples of alternatives that are working, see: Starke, L. 1990. *Signs of Hope: Working Towards Our Common Future.* Oxford: Oxford University Press. Ekins, P. 1992. *A New World Order: Grassroots Movements for Global Change.* London: Routledge. Schmidheiny, S. 1992. *Changing Course: A Global Business Perspective on Development and the Environment.* Cambridge, MA: The M. I. T. Press. Goldberg, J.; Johansson, T. B.; Reddy, A. K.; and Williams, R. H. "Basic Needs and Much More With One Kilowatt Per Capita." *Ambio.* vol. 14. no. 4-5. pp. 190-200.

53 Linden, E. "Megacities." *Time.* 11 January 1993. pp. 30-31. Margolis, M. 1992. World Monitor. March 1992. pp. 42-50.

54 Finnbogadóttir, V. 8 April 1992. Personal communication.

55 Few people realize how common terrorist bombings have become in the United States. See: Thomas, P. 1993. "Use of Explosives in Crimes Doubles Since 1987, Killing Two Dozen a Year." *The Washington Post.* 13 March 1993. p. A3.

56 Meadows, D. H.; Meadows, D. L.; and Randers, J. 1992. *Beyond the Limits.* Post Mill, VT: Chelsea Green Publishing. p. 196.

57 The suggested actions presented here have been drawn from many sources including: Goodland, R. and Daly, H. "Ten Reasons Why Northern Income

Growth is not the Solution to Southern Poverty." In: *International Journal of Sustainable Development* 1 (2) 23-30, 1992. Serageldin, I. "Agriculture and Environmentally Sustainable Development." *Bank's World*. April 1993. pp. 18-21. Peccei, A. 1977. *The Human Quality*. Oxford: Pergamon; The World Commission on Environment and Development. 1987. *Our Common Future*. Oxford: Oxford University Press. Demeny, P. 1992. "Policies Seeking a Reduction of High Fertility: A Case for the Demand Side." ESD/P/ICPD.1994/EG.II/INF.16. New York: Population Division of the United Nations. MacNeill, J.; Winsemius, P.; and Yakushiji, T. *Beyond Interdependence*. Oxford: Oxford University Press. Brown, L. R.; Flavin, C.; and Postel, S. 1991. *Saving the Planet*. New York: Norton. Secretariat, U. N. Conference on Environment and Development. 1992. *Agenda 21*. Oxford: Oxford University Press. Korten, D. C. 1990. *Getting to the 21st Century: Voluntary Action and the Global Agenda*. Hartford, CT: Kumarian Press. Brown, L. R. 1981. *Building a Sustainable Society*. New York: Norton; Brown, L. R., et al. 1990. *State of the World 1990*. New York: Norton.

[58]   Gore, A. "What Is Wrong With Us?" *Time*. 2 January 1989. p. 66. Wilson, E. O. "Is Humanity Suicidal?" *The New York Times Magazine*. 30 May 1993. p. 24.

[59]   Rev. 21:4.

[60]   Berry, T. 1988. *The Dream of the Earth*. San Francisco: Sierra Club Books. p. 29.

[61]   Berry, T. 1988. op. cit. p. 153.

[62]   The World Commission on Environment and Development. 1987. *Our Common Future*. Oxford: Oxford University Press. McNeill, J. "Strategies for Sustainable Economic Development." *Scientific American*. September 1989. pp. 154-165.

[63]   The attribute of "replicability" is an important aspect of sustainability. It invites the North to live in a way that would be sustainable *globally* if the North's lifestyle were replicated throughout the South, too. For further information on this concept, see: Corea, G. "The Rich Must Show the Way to a Replicable Lifestyle." *South Letter*. June 1991. p. 15.

[64]   McNamara, R. S. 1991. *A Global Population Policy to Advance Human Development in the 21st Century: Rafael M. Salas Memorial Lecture*. New York: United Nations. pp. 15-16. Goodland, R. 1991. "The Case That the World Has Reached Limits." In: Goodland, R.; Daly, H.; and El Serafy, S., eds. 1991. *Environmentally Sustainable Economic Development Building on Brundtland: Environment Working Paper No. 46*. Washington: The World Bank. Vitousek, P. M.; Ehrlich, P. R.; Ehrlich, A. H.; and Matson, P. A. "Human Appropriation of the Products of Photosynthesis." *Bioscience*. May 1986.

[65]   Anderson, J. W. and More, M. 1993 "Born Oppressed." In *The Washington Post*. Washington: *The Washington Post*. 14 February 1993. p. A1.

[66]   Berry, T. 1988. *The Dream of the Earth*. San Francisco: Sierra Club Books. p. 37.

67 A short, thoughtful analysis of the U.N. Conference on Environment and Development in the context of the decline of the Westphalian system of international order is provided in Suter, K. 1992. "Toward a More Equitable World Order." An unpublished paper prepared for the Kuala Lumpur Conference of the Club of Rome. 15-19 November 1992. Available from K. Suter, GPO Box 4878, Sydney, NSW, 2001, Australia.

68 An unusually candid portrait of the problems in the United Nations is provided in Thornburgh, D. 1 March 1993. *Report to the Secretary General of the United Nations by the Under Secretary-General for Administration and Management.* New York: United Nations.

69 Binder, D. and Crossette, B. 1993. "As Ethnic Wars Multiply, U.S. Strives for a Policy." *The New York Times.* 7 February 1993. P. A1.

70 Fischer, L. 1954. *Gandhi: His Life and Message for the World.* New York: Mentor Books. pp. 100-101.

71 Sharp, G. 1985. *National Security Through Civilian-Based Defense.* Omaha, NE: The Association for Transarmament Studies.

72 Schmidheiny, Stephan, et al. 1992. *Changing Course: A Global Business Perspective on Development and the Environment.* Cambridge, MA: The MIT Press.

73 See Grossman, R. L. and Adams, F. T. *Taking Care of Business: Citizenship and the Charter of Incorporation.* Cambridge MA 02140 (P. O. Box 806): Charter, Ink./CSPP. 1993.

74 One that is far above average is: General Assembly of the Presbyterian Church (U.S.A.) 1990. *Restoring Creation for Ecology and Justice.* Louisville, KY: Presbyterian Church (U.S.A.), and an associated study guide: Presbyterian Eco-Justice Task Force. 1989. *Keeping and Healing the Creation.* Louisville, KY: Presbyterian Church (U.S.A.). Others that are more disappointing include: John Paul II, His Holiness. 1990. "Peace with God the Creator, Peace with All of Creation: A Message for the Celebration of the World Day of Peace, 1 January 1990." Rome: The Vatican; and John Paul II, His Holiness. 1991. "Centesimus Annus." Rome: The Vatican.

75 Kinnamon, M., ed. 1991. *Signs of the Spirit: Official Report of the Seventh Assembly.* Geneva: WCC Publications. pp. 68-69.

76 Ramphal, S. 1992. *Our Country, The Planet: Forging A Partnership for Survival.* Washington: Island Press. pp. 202-203.

77 From an evolutionary point of view, there are many interesting questions about how and when early humans became aware of the divine or began to hear or sense revelations. One examination of this matter that I have found very helpful and insightful is: Jaynes, J. 1976. *The Origin of Consciousness in the Breakdown of the Bicameral Mind.* Boston: Houghton Mifflin Company.

78 Binder, D. and Crossette, B. 1993 "As Ethnic Wars Multiply, U.S. Strives for a Policy." *The New York Times.* 7 February 1993. p. A1 Romans 8: 18-24.

[79] Romans 8: 18-24.

[80] Genesis: 1: 28-30.

[81] An Earth-future without humans is really not an Earth-future. Without humans, the loss of potential and consciousness would be so large that Earth would simply not be Earth. Furthermore, an Earth- future without humans is impossible for humans even to imagine. For a thoughtful attempt to imagine an Earth-future without humans, see Schell, J. 1982. "The Second Death." In Schell, J. *The Fate of the Earth*. New York: A. Knopf. pp. 99-178.

[82] The original article was written by Branimir Talajic, a Sarajevo-based reporter for *Novi Vjesnik*, a daily newspaper in Zagreb. His article was translated for Pacific News Service by Branimir and Yelka Talajic, Croatian immigrants who live in Saratoga, California. Reprinted by permission.

[83] For a list of the 48 religious and ethnic wars now in progress on every continent, see: Binder, D. and Crossette, B. "As Ethnic Wars Multiply, U.S. Strives for a Policy." *The New York Times*. 7 February 1993. p. A1.

[84] See Swimme, B. and Berry, T. 1992. *The Universe Story*. Cloud, P. *Oasis in Space: A History of the Planet from the Beginning*. Cambridge: Cambridge University Press; Capra, F. and Steindl-Rast, D. *Belonging to the Universe*. San Francisco: Harper-Collins; and Wilson, E. O. 1992. *The Diversity of Life*. Cambridge, MA: Belknap Press of Harvard University Press; and Crosby, A. W. 1986. *Ecological Imperialism: The Biological Expansion of Europe, 900-1900*. Cambridge: Cambridge University Press.

[85] While no faith tradition has gone very far in developing inter- species ethics and morality, a few individuals have made significant steps in this direction. See, for example: Engel, J. R., and Engel, J. G., eds. 1990. *Ethics of Environment and Development: Global Challenge and International Response*. University of Arizona Press. Pinches, C. and McDaniel, J. B., eds. 1993. *Good News for Animals: Christian Approaches to Animal Well-Being*. Maryknoll, NY: Orbis Books.

[86] For examples of questions being raised by others, see: Union of Concerned Scientists. 1992. "World Scientists' Warning to Humanity." (This statement signed by 1,575 scientists from 69 countries and a press release are available from Union of Concerned Scientists, 1616 P Street, NW, Suite 310, Washington, DC, 20036, USA.) Lasch, C. "Is Progress Obsolete?" *Beyond the Year 2000: A Special Issue*. Time. Fall 1992. p. 71. International Coordinating Committee on Religion and Earth. 1993. "An Earth Charter: A Spiritual Perspective." Available from: International Coordinating Committee on Religion and the Earth, P.O. Box 67, Greenwich, CT 06831, USA. Kyser, R. 1993. "The Role of the Churches in Population Growth, Immigration and the Environment." 1993. *The Social Contract*. Winter 1992-93. pp. 75-142. Goodland, R. 1991. *Tropical Deforestation Solutions, Ethics, and Religions: Environment Working Paper No. 43*. Washington: The World Bank. Goodland; R., Daly, H.; and El Serafy, S. 1991. *Environmentally Sustainable Economic Development Building on Brundtland: Environment Working Paper No. 46*. Washington: The World Bank. Forrester, J. W. 1971. "Churches at the

Transition Between Growth and World Equilibrium." In: Forrester, J. W. 1975. *Collected Papers of Jay W. Forrester.* Cambridge, MA: The M. I. T. Press. pp. 255-269. Shiva, V. 1989. *Staying Alive: Women, Ecology, and Development.* London: Zed Books. Spretnak, C. 1991. *States of Grace: The Recovery of Meaning in the Postmodern Age.* San Francisco: Harper Collins. Hardin, G. 1963. "A Second Sermon on the Mount." *Perspectives in Biology and Medicine.* vol. vi, no. 3, Spring 1963. Hardin, G. 1968. "The Tragedy of the Commons." *Science.* vol. 162. 13 December 1968. pp. 1243-1248. Vickers, G. 1970. *Freedom in a Rocking Boat: Changing Values in an Unstable Society.* Middlesex, England: Pelican Books. Linden, E. "Too Many People." *Beyond the Year 2000: A Special Issue.* Time. Fall 1992. pp. 64-65.

[87] Professor Julian Jaynes at Princeton University argues that "revelation" (hearing the gods) is a capability that humans have largely lost since the founding of the great religious traditions. Those few that still hear "voices" are largely dismissed by society as having one form or another of mental illness. See: Jaynes, J. 1976. *The Origins of Consciousness in the Breakdown of the Bicameral Mind.* Boston: Houghton Mifflin Company.

[88] Aykroyd, P. H. 1992. *The Anniversary Compulsion.* Toronto: Dundurn Press.

[89] 1992. "A Fast Journey to 2 Celebrations." *The New York Times.* 29 November 1992. Section 5, p. 3.

[90] *Beyond the Year 2000: What to Expect in the New Millennium: A Special Issue.* 1992. New York: Time.

[91] Boorstin, D. J. 1983. *The Discoverers.* New York: Random House. pp. 596-603.

[92] Several thoughtful books and papers have now been published relating to how we humans might mark Earth's entry into the 21st century. These include: Aykroyd, P. H. 1992. *The Anniversary Compulsion.* Toronto: Dundurn Press. Schwartz, H. 1990. *Century's End: A Cultural History of the Fin de Siècle from the 990s through the 1990s.* New York: Doubleday. Hyde, L. 1979. *The Gift.* New York: Vintage Books. Johnson, W. M. 1991. Celebrations. New Brunswick: Transaction Publishers.

[93] John Paul II, His Holiness. 1992. "Lessons of the Galileo Case." Origins: CNS *Documentary Service.* 12 November 1992. pp. 370-373.

[94] Berry, T. 1988. *The Dream of the Earth.* San Francisco: Sierra Club Books. p. 137.

PART TWO

Shaping A Global, Spiritually Informed Ethic

A Call to Our Guiding Institutions

The Message of the Parliament of the World's Religions
Draft One, September 1998

From the Global Ethic to a Call to Our Guiding Institutions

Introduction

At defining moments in history, great challenges arise and, at the same time, great opportunities emerge. Each such moment is shaped by the critical issues which must be addressed and by the resources upon which the human community can draw.

Today, widespread recognition that the world is a global village is reaffirming several ancient verities. We human beings are interdependent and responsible for the care of the Earth and of all life. We are ourselves worthy of meaningful lives and obliged to care for the entire human family. The choices that will shape a just and peaceful future are choices that we must make together.

Unique to this moment is the possibility of a new level of creative engagement between the world's religious and spiritual communities and the other powerful institutions that influence the character and course of human society. As religion and spirituality find new ways to cooperate with government, business and commerce, education, and media, an unprecedented process of transformation can begin to unfold. Therefore, what is needed now is a persuasive invitation to these guiding institutions that will encourage new partnerships in building a better world.

At this special moment—at the threshold of a new century and a new millennium, and on the occasion of the 1999 Parliament of the World's Religions in Cape Town, South Africa—the Council for a Parliament of the World's Religions (CPWR) offers such an invitation, in the form of this document, *A Call to Our Guiding Institutions.*

Earth cannot be changed for the better unless the consciousness of individuals is changed first. We pledge to increase our awareness by disciplining our minds, by meditation, by prayer, or by positive thinking. Without risk and a readiness to sacrifice there can be no fundamental change in our situation. Therefore we commit ourselves to this global ethic, to understanding one another, and to socially beneficial, peace-fostering, and nature-friendly ways of life.

We invite all people, whether religious or not, to do the same.

Towards a Global Ethic:
An Initial Declaration,
1993 Parliament of the World's
Religions, Chicago

Continuing the Parliament Tradition

The 1999 Parliament of the World's Religions and this *Call* continue a tradition born in Chicago. The tradition began in 1893 at the first Parliament of Religions, when several hundred leaders, scholars, and other representatives of the world religions came together to think about the place of religion in the modern world.

This tradition was reborn in Chicago in 1993 as more than 7000 people from a wide spectrum of the world's religions gathered again in Chicago. They came together to explore issues of personal and communal religious identity, to engage in thoughtful dialogue with persons of other cultures and traditions, and to discover new ways of bringing the attention, energy, and influence of religion and spirituality to bear on the critical issues confronting the planetary community.

Throughout the 1993 Parliament, all participants were challenged to think urgently, critically, and holistically about the role of religion in the search for creative solutions to the world's most pressing problems. In this context, the 1993 Parliament offered an inspirational and thoughtful statement of fundamental ethical principles shared by the world's religious and spiritual traditions.

That statement took form in an extraordinary document, *Towards a Global Ethic: An Initial Declaration.* This ground-breaking work, signed by nearly two hundred world religious and spiritual leaders gathered in Chicago, set forth four fundamental commitments—to a culture of Non-Violence and Respect for Life, of Solidarity and a Just Economic Order, of Tolerance and a Life of Truthfulness, and of Equal Rights and Partnership between Men and Women. Each of these commitments is unquestionably relevant in the face of the issues which the Parliament addressed. As a consequence, the *Global Ethic* has been hailed by many as one of the most evocative declarations of its kind.

How can the principles and the commitments of the Global Ethic be directly related to the functioning of the institutions that exercise the greatest power in society?

The Next Step

At the convening of the 1999 Parliament, the Council for a Parliament of the World's Religions urges continuing reflection on the commitments at the heart of the *Global Ethic,* and an effort to apply them more broadly. Essential to such an effort is the recognition that we live in a world in which powerful institutions exercise a major influence on our collective future. Inherent in the defining documents and traditions of these institutions are values and methods, which should be examined in the light of the principles of the *Global Ethic*. In other words, how can the principles and the commitments of the *Global Ethic* be directly related to the functioning of the institutions that exercise the greatest power in society? How might the Parliament process of creative engagement come to involve not only the religions of the world, but also other guiding institutions—government, business and commerce, education, and the media?

In Cape Town, in 1999, the Council for a Parliament of the World's Religions offers a new document. *A Call to Our Guiding Institutions* is addressed to the world's most influential and powerful institutions, asking them to examine their roles for a new century and a new millennium, in the light of the declaration *Towards a Global Ethic*.

It is the hope of the Council that the *Call* will also provide encouragement and direction for those wishing to offer gifts of service to the world. To give such a gift is to express a fundamental spiritual inclination towards generosity, caring, hospitality, compassion, and good will. In fact, the existence of goodness in the world has often been directly related to the giving of such gifts and the spirit in which they are given. Though ambitious endeavors and noble institutions have made undeniable contributions, the world continues to thirst for such individual and collective gifts of service—now, more than ever.

The Nature of the Call

A Call to Our Guiding Institutions is not a "call" in the familiar sense of a prescriptive or admonitory document. The authority of the *Call* will come not from its endorsement by religious and spiritual leaders, although it is hoped that it will be endorsed by many. The *Call* is an invitation to dialogue about the creation of a peaceful, just, and sustainable future for the whole of the Earth community. For this reason, it is cast in the form of challenging questions rather than declarations or injunctions. Its strength will flow from its expression of beliefs and convictions already deeply held—and held in common—by the world's great religious and spiritual communities.

In the pages that follow, the four key commitments of *Towards a Global Ethic: An Initial Declaration*, as well as key excerpts from that document, appear in the margins of the various sections. This serves as a reminder that the *Global Ethic* sets the stage for the *Call* and shapes its core—the vital questions addressed to each of several guiding institutions.

We invite each of the world's major institutions and all thoughtful persons and organizations to reflect on these questions and to respond in the ways that seem to them most appropriate.

The Council for a Parliament of the World's Religions, 1999 Parliament, Cape Town, South Africa

Rationale

Visions of the World

Visions of the world as it might be have found expression in the world's religious and spiritual traditions—traditions that embody human aspirations for meaning and purpose in life; respect and mutuality between diverse peoples, cultures, and religions; the pursuit of justice and peace; alleviation of suffering; and harmony with the Earth.

Today there is heightened spiritual movement toward the realization of these visions. Encounters between peoples of different religious, spiritual, and cultural traditions create new possibilities for establishing ethical common ground. This new awareness of shared ethical principles marks the first step into a new era of creative engagement between the world's guiding institutions—religion, government, business and commerce, education, and media. Creative engagement is the discovery and implementation of new modes of outreach, cooperation, and constructive common action among these institutions. The call to such engagement in the face of unprecedented challenges to the well-being of the planetary community is the harbinger of a new day.

Towards a Global Ethic

While the world's great religious and spiritual traditions differ profoundly with respect to beliefs and practices, they nevertheless acknowledge in common certain ancient ethical principles. One formulation of this ethical common ground is found in the document, *Towards a Global Ethic: An Initial Declaration,* issued on the occasion of the 1993 Parliament of the World's Religions.

The document identifies four universal directives that offer a basis for a "global ethic." The four directives are:

- Do not kill.
- Do not steal.

- Do not lie.
- Do not commit sexual immorality.

These directives are then described and understood in the following affirmations:

- Have respect for life.
- Deal honestly and fairly.
- Speak and act truthfully.
- Respect and love one another.

Towards a Global Ethic then proposes that these affirmations lead to four vital commitments (listed here with excerpts from the text in quotation marks):

• Commitment to a Culture of Non-Violence and Respect for Life.

"All people have a right to life, safety, and the free development of personality insofar as they do not injure the rights of others."

"To be authentically human in the spirit of our great religious and ethical traditions means that in public as well as private life we must be concerned for others and ready to help.... Every people, every race, every religion must show tolerance and respect—indeed, high appreciation—for every other."

• Commitment to a Culture of Solidarity and a Just Economic Order.

"No one has the right to rob or dispossess in any way whatsoever any other person or the commonweal.... No one has the right to use her or his possessions without concern for the needs of society and Earth."

"We must utilize economic and political power for service to humanity instead of misusing it in ruthless battles for domination. We must develop a spirit of compassion with those who suffer, with special care for the children, the aged, the poor, the disabled, the refugees, and the lonely."

• Commitment to a Culture of Tolerance and a Life of Truthfulness.

"No woman or man, no institution, no state or church or religious community has the right to speak lies to other humans."

"We must cultivate truthfulness in all our relationships instead of dishonesty, dissembling, and opportunism.... We must courageously serve the truth and we must remain constant and trustworthy, instead of yielding to opportunistic accommodation to life."

- **Commitment to a Culture of Equal Rights and Partnership between Men and Women.**

"No one has the right to degrade others to mere sex objects, to lead them into or hold them in sexual dependency."

"The relationship between women and men should be characterized not by patronizing behavior or exploitation, but by love, partnership, and trustworthiness."

These commitments have significant implications for the inner life of individuals and the shared life of the human community.

First, "...they can provide what obviously cannot be attained by economic plans, political programs, or legal regulations alone: A change in the inner orientation, the whole mentality, the `hearts' of people, and a conversion from a false path to a new orientation for life."

Second, the four commitments suggest the outlines of "...a vision of peoples living peacefully together, of ethnic and ethical groupings and of religions sharing responsibility for the care of Earth...," a vision made possible by our new awareness of ethical common ground.

Creative Engagement

When reflecting on the future of the human community, one must consider the world's most powerful institutions, institutions that influence nearly every aspect of life on the planet. For better and for worse, these institutions have played and will continue to play guiding roles, making decisions which affect the most basic functioning of the Earth's systems and of all life.

Clearly, the critical issues facing the world today offer an unprecedented ethical challenge to these institutions. The state of the world can be improved only if shared ethical principles shape and direct the course of the guiding institutions in the twenty-first century. In fact, what is most urgently needed is an opening to a new kind of creative engagement

—the exploration of a new vision of possible futures and the discovery of new ways for the world's guiding institutions to work together.

Addressing the Critical Issues

The confluence of universal aspirations with the realities of the world situation set the critical issues of our time in stark relief. Addressing these issues from the perspective of a shared "global ethic," gives rise to a variety of responses offering transformation and hope. What follows is a list of several possible responses.

• Building Community

Diversity is a hallmark of our modern experience. Today, every metropolitan center is home to a striking variety of cultures, nationalities, races, and religions. Never before has the encounter between people from different paths and perspectives been so widespread, touching the lives of individuals and communities across the planet, and recasting the dynamics of our world. When such encounters take place in an atmosphere of respect and mutuality, then new understanding, cooperation, and enrichment will result. Sadly, however—and even more evident today—are the difficulties that diversity presents. Inevitably, tensions, hostilities, and violence arise from misunderstanding, fear, and hatred of those who differ from us. As a consequence, we are faced with the urgent task of approaching diversity in such a way that differences are no longer barriers but rather bridges to harmonious and vibrant community.

• Commitment to Sustainability

Today the human family numbers nearly six billion. Our total population is likely to approach and even to exceed the limits of the Earth's ability to support us. Economic analysis suggests that to meet even the basic needs of a significantly larger population would require an exponential increase in the world's economy, prompting thoughtful persons to ask whether the Earth can possibly sustain such demands. For example, already one-half of all land has been transformed for human use, levels of atmospheric carbon dioxide have dramatically risen, and one-half of all accessible fresh water has been claimed to meet current human needs. As a result, 1 out of every 8 plants and ever greater numbers of animals are at risk of extinction, a situation which further imperils the

planet's human community. The challenge is to find sustainable ways
to peacefully meet the needs of all people while preserving the whole
community of life on Earth.

• Striving for Justice

Currently, four-fifths of the world's people live on $1 per day or less.
Wrenching poverty, exacerbated by unfair distribution of resources,
gives rise to disease, crime, violence, systemic injustice, and hopeless-
ness. Whether from an idealistic or a pragmatic point of view, it is clear
that this situation is intolerable. To ignore the sufferings of a majority
of the human community is morally untenable as well as economically,
politically, and socially unwise. Injustice of this kind and scope poisons
the social, moral, and spiritual life of all of us. Therefore to imagine that
there can be peace without justice is dangerously wrong.

• Solidarity and Service

The principal obstacle to the pursuit of justice is the absence of an
awareness of our fundamental connection to one another. The divisions
of the world—into rich and poor, North and South, men and women,
privileged and disenfranchised, privileged and exploited—exacerbates
this pervasive alienation. The only remedy for this condition is compassionate identification with others, with their joys and sorrows, their
sufferings and struggles. Solidarity is the root of justice and the well-
spring of service. In solidarity we realize our shared humanness and
in service to one another we emerge from our estrangement and our
brokenness is healed.

• Seeking Spiritual Grounding

Each of the world's great religious and spiritual traditions speaks elo-
quently to the aspirations enumerated here and each offers pathways to
their fulfillment. To be sure, religious and spiritual traditions have often
been distorted and misused, with destructive results. Nevertheless, it is
becoming clear that without a grounding in spirituality, these visions of
the world as it might be cannot be realized.

The world's great religious and spiritual traditions offer the wisdom to move beyond our narrow self-interest, and the inspiration to build community in the spirit of hospitality.

The world's great religious and spiritual traditions offer the wisdom to recognize the interdependence of all life and the systems that support it, and the resolve to choose sustainable ways of living.

The world's great religious and spiritual traditions offer the wisdom to see that the needs of the other make a claim on our lives and our energies, and the courage to struggle for justice and peace.

The world's great religious and spiritual traditions offer the wisdom to remember our place in the human family, and the compassion that finds expression in service.

A CALL TO OUR GUIDING INSTITUTIONS

Preamble

As human beings

At a time of great challenges and great opportunities, the Council for a Parliament of the World's Religions respectfully calls upon the world's guiding institutions to reassess and redefine their roles in the next century and the next millennium.

...we are, each of us, interdependent, and we must deal with each other peaceably and respectfully;

... we are all—children, women, men—worthy of a meaningful life and we must treat all with kindness, fairness, and encouragement;

...we are everyone responsible for the care of the Earth on which we depend and the well-being of the communities in which we live;

...apart and together, we see that our futures will be shaped by the extent to which we link our societies with a global ethic in partnerships that reach across the continents and across cultural, ethnic, racial, economic, social, political, and religious lines.

As religious and spiritual persons

... we center our lives in an Ultimate Reality, drawing hope there-from, in trust or vision, in prayer or meditation, in word or silence.

...we seek Creative Engagement with each of the great institutions that so profoundly influence all life on Earth. We call on religious and spiritual individuals, communities, groups, and organizations to find new ways to cooperate with government, business and commerce, education, and media to address the critical issues that confront the human community.

....we commit to courses of action that can reasonably and constructively be followed well into the future, on behalf of succeeding generations.

Together, we affirm

...the four fundamental commitments, which stood at the center of *Towards a Global Ethic: An Initial Declaration.*
1. Commitment to a Culture of Non-Violence and Respect for Life.
2. Commitment to a Culture of Solidarity and a Just Economic Order.

3. Commitment to a Culture of Tolerance and a Life of Truthfulness.
4. Commitment to a Culture of Equal Rights and Partnership between Men and Women.

Together, we extend this Call

...to the guiding institutions whose decisions will mean so much to the future of the entire community of the Earth, to religion, to government, to business and commerce, to education, and to the media.

THE CALL TO RELIGION

We envision a world

...in which wisdom and compassion are prized,
...in which service is seen as one of the most essential of all religious acts,
...in which the religious and spiritual communities exist in harmony,
...in which peace and justice prevail, and
...in which the sacredness of the Earth and of all life is everywhere acknowledged.

Among the noblest functions of religion is the binding together of one person to another through systems of beliefs, practices, and ethics— centered in an Ultimate Reality, however understood—that honor at once the humanity and dignity of each person and the vital importance of community.

On the occasion of the 1999 Parliament of the World Religions, convened in Cape Town, South Africa, the Council for a Parliament of the World's Religions calls upon the world's religious and spiritual traditions to offer new gifts to the world and its people.

At a time of great challenges and great opportunities, we respectfully ask that religious and spiritual individuals, communities, groups, and organizations reassess and redefine their roles in the next century and the next millennium.

A fundamental demand: Every human being must be treated humanely.

This principle implies very concrete standards to which we humans should hold firm. From it arise four broad, ancient guidelines for human behavior, which are found in most religions of the world.

1. Commitment to a Culture of Non-violence and Respect for Life.

2. Commitment to a Culture of Solidarity and a Just Economic Order.

3. Commitment to a Culture of Tolerance and a Life of Truthfulness.

4. Commitment to a Culture of Equal Rights and Partnership Between Men and Women.

Towards a Global Ethic:

An Initial Declaration

We ask that within each tradition an urgent and deliberate effort be made to create and implement new modes of creative engagement between religion and the other great institutions whose decisions bear so strongly on the whole of the planetary community. By "creative engagement", we mean the exploration of a new vision of possible futures and the discovery and implementation of new modes of outreach, cooperation, and constructive common action.

In particular, we ask that within each tradition the following questions be addressed with the deep care and reflection that can lead to new resolve and new initiative.

1   How can the world's religious and spiritual communities bring their teachings on peace and justice to bear more directly on their engagement with the other guiding institutions and thereby make these teachings more widely known and more influential in the lives of Earth's people?

2   What can religions do now to prevent religious belief from functioning as a source of intolerance, conflict, and violence?

    How might religious and spiritual individuals, communities, and institutions commit to a future course of peace, justice, and non-violent resolution of disputes?

3   How can each tradition most effectively and most immediately demonstrate its respect for other traditions? How are we to build urgently needed bridges between and among religious and spiritual traditions, communities, and leaders?

4   How best can religious people work together, within and across traditions, to respond directly to the critical issues (including violence, racism, injustice, ecological degradation, and the systematic deprivation and exploitation of women and children) which confront us all?

    How best can the world's religions make themselves heard concerning these most urgent issues?

5   How might the religions engage with government, business and commerce, education, and the media to ensure that the sacredness of the Earth is recognized and understood as a religious and spiritual reality?

6 How can the world's religious and spiritual traditions most effectively promote service to the human family—especially to the poor and vulnerable—and to the Earth as an affirmation of their teachings of compassion, service, personal spiritual growth, and life lived in ever deepening relationship to ultimate reality?

THE CALL TO BUSINESS AND COMMERCE

We envision a world

    ...in which the productive activities of humans are creative and vital,
    ...in which commercial exchange is just, harmonious, and culturally enriching, and
    ...in which we meet the essential needs of all in a manner that can be sustained well into the future

Among the noblest functions of business and commerce is the invention, production, or location of substantial, renewable, and non-disruptive means to meet the basic physical and social needs of each human community.

On the occasion of the 1999 Parliament of the World's Religions, convened in Cape Town, South Africa, the Council for a Parliament of the World's Religions calls upon the institutions of business and commerce to offer new gifts to the world and its people.

At a time of great challenges and great opportunities, we respectfully ask that individuals, communities, groups, and organizations involved in business, finance, trade, agriculture, and commerce reassess and redefine their roles in the next century and the next millennium.

We ask that within the world's business and commerce community an urgent and deliberate effort be made to create and implement new modes of creative engagement with religion and the other great institutions whose decisions bear so strongly on the whole of the planetary community. By "creative engagement," we mean the exploration of a new vision of possible futures and the discovery and implementation of new modes of outreach, cooperation, and constructive common action.

No new global order without a new global ethic!

We women and men of various religions and regions of Earth therefore address all people, religious and non-religious. We wish to express the following convictions we hold in common:

• We all have a responsibility for a better global order.

• Our involvement for the sake of human rights, freedom, justice, peace, and the preservation of the Earth is absolutely necessary.

• Our different religious and cultural traditions must not prevent our common involvement in opposing all forms of inhumanity and working for greater humaneness.

The principles expressed in this Global Ethic can be affirmed by all persons with ethical convictions, whether religiously grounded or not.

Towards a Global Ethic:

An Initial Declaration

In particular, we ask that within each sector of the institutions of business and commerce the following questions be addressed with the deep care and reflection that can lead to new resolve and new initiative.

1 How might business and commerce develop and extend a common statement of ethical standards in business that would be accepted and implemented around the world?

2 How can business and commerce come best to understand and address the long-term negative effects of patterns of production and especially their often harmful impact on communities?

3 How can business and commerce most immediately and thoroughly integrate the principles of social and economic justice, such that there are fair wages and working conditions for all, and such that the world no longer must bear the scourge of child labor, prison labor, sweatshops, and virtual slavery?

4 How can business and commerce work creatively with other guiding institutions to develop a greater sensitivity within the corporate environment to the dangerous realities of uncontrolled human consumption?

5 How can business and commerce bring their collective experience and their strategies for innovation into partnerships with groups and organizations—e.g., non governmental organizations (NGOs)—now working for peace, justice, interreligious understanding and ecological sustainability?

6 How can business and commerce enable all peoples and nations to participate equally in the global market and thus promote a level economic field among nations?

7 How can the world of business and commerce expand its fundamental goals to include not only the increase of wealth but also the elimination of poverty.

THE CALL TO GOVERNMENT

We envision a world

> ... in which the richness of Earth's diverse cultures is recognized by all,
> ... in which enduring responsibilities derived from fundamental ethical and moral principles are taken on without reserve,
> ... in which universal human rights are recognized and upheld,
> ... in which peace is the rule and not the exception, and
> ... in which the great decisions in human affairs are made with a thoughtful care for the future of the planetary community.

Among the noblest functions of government is the assurance of individual and collective well-being and of the social and political integrity of the community, through the interplay of individual freedoms and collective action.

On the occasion of the 1999 Parliament of the World Religions, convened in Cape Town, South Africa, the Council for a Parliament of the World's Religions calls upon the institution of government to offer new gifts to the world and its people.

At a time of great challenges and great opportunities, we respectfully ask that individuals, communities, groups, and organizations involved in government at every level reassess and redefine their roles in the next century and the next millennium.

We ask that within the world's governments an urgent and deliberate effort be made to create and implement new modes of creative engagement with religion and the other great institutions whose decisions bear so strongly on the whole of the planetary community. By "creative engagement," we mean the exploration of a new vision of possible futures and the discovery and implementation of new modes of outreach, cooperation, and constructive common action.

In such a dramatic global situation humanity needs a vision of peoples living peacefully together, of ethnic and ethical groupings and of religions sharing responsibility for the care of Earth.

A vision rests on hopes, goals, ideals, and standards. But all over the world these have slipped from our hands. Yet we are convinced that, despite their frequent abuses and failures, it is the communities of faith who bear a responsibility to demonstrate that such hopes, ideals, and standards can be guarded, grounded, and lived.

This is especially true in the modern state.

Guarantees of freedom of conscience and religion are necessary but they do not substitute for binding values, convictions, and norms which are valid for all humans regardless of their social origin, sex, skin color, language, or religion.

Towards a Global Ethic:

An Initial Declaration

In particular, we ask that within each sector of the institution of government the following questions be addressed with the deep care and reflection that can lead to new resolve and new initiative.

1 How can creative engagement with religion and the other guiding institutions assist in fostering dialogue within government and within society on spiritual, moral, social, and ethical values?

2 How can individuals and agencies within government creatively engage with religion and other institutions to support the realization of universal human rights—in particular, the rights of women, children, and the poor?

3 How can governments—most urgently and effectively, individually and in concert—denounce, counter, and prevent genocide, as well as race- or culture-based and/or religiously inspired oppression?

4 How can government at all levels assist in the development and nurture of cultures of peace throughout the world and, in particular:
a) eliminate the use of land mines and government sales of arms, and
b) support the development of peace studies and peace action programs?

5 How can government at every level most urgently and effectively encourage and implement sustainable ways of living in a vital yet fragile world?

6 How can the governments of the world work together to move beyond the present model of balanced power among nation states toward a model of cooperation within the family of nations?

THE CALL TO EDUCATION

We envision a world

... in which learning, as one of the most important pursuits of the human family, is made available to all,

... in which ethical, moral, and spiritual questions are part of civil and international discourse,

... in which each religious and spiritual tradition, each racial and ethnic group, and each culture becomes familiar to and appreciated by every other, thus fostering harmony among the members of the human community,

... in which every human being grows steadily in personal responsibility and committed service to the entire community of life, and

... in which the vital, fragile, and sacred Earth is cherished by all.

Among the noblest functions of education is the discovery of enduring and imaginative ways to translate and then to question humanity's knowledge, skills, traditions, travails, and insights so that the members of each successive generation may be well-equipped to lead reflective, honorable, and engaged lives which enrich their respective communities.

On the occasion of the 1999 Parliament of the World Religions, convened in Cape Town, South Africa, the Council for a Parliament of the World's Religions calls upon the institution of education to offer new gifts to the world and its people.

At a time of great challenges and great opportunities, we respectfully ask that educators at all levels, the schools in which they labor, and the publishers who distribute their materials reassess and redefine their roles in the next century and the next millennium.

We ask that within the world's educational establishments an urgent and deliberate effort be made to create and implement new modes of creative engagement with religion and the other great institutions whose decisions bear so strongly on the whole of the planetary community. By "creative engagement," we mean the exploration of a new vision of possible futures and the discovery and implementation of new modes of outreach, cooperation, and constructive common action.

Every human being without distinction of age, sex, race, skin color, physical or mental ability, language, religion, political view, or national or social origin possesses an inalienable and untouchable dignity. And everyone, the individual as well as the state is, therefore, obliged to honor this dignity and protect it.

Human beings must always be the subjects of rights, must be ends, never mere means, never objects of commercialization and industrialization in economics, politics and media, in research institutes, and industrial corporations...

There is a principle that is found and has persisted in many religious and ethical traditions of humankind for thousands of years:

What you do not wish done to yourself, do not do to others.

Or in positive terms: **What you wish done to yourself, do to others.**

This should be the irrevocable, unconditional norm for all areas of life, for families and communities, for races, nations, and religions.

Towards a Global Ethic:

An Initial Declaration

In particular, we ask that within each sector of the institution of education the following questions be addressed with the deep care and reflection that can lead to new resolve and new initiative.

1 How can educators best reach out to the world's poorest and least educated?

 In the outreach to the world's poor, how can the best use be made of growing understanding of the different modes of human learning?

2 How can educators make the best use of new media and new technologies to broaden intercultural access and exchange?

 How can education have the most positive impact in areas of vital concern, such as literacy, sanitation, parenting, and enrichment of the lives of women and children?

3 How can the guiding institutions work together to secure education in peace, non-violence, and respect for other religions and ways of life in every culture and from the earliest ages?

4 What are the most effective steps that can be taken to assure that one of the central elements of curriculum at all levels involves the inquiry into the most basic human survival needs and what it takes for the human family to survive on a healthy planet?

5 What can most quickly and most usefully be done to enrich the world-wide education of girls and women?

THE CALL TO MEDIA

We envision a world

... in which the stories which matter most are those which enrich understanding, deepen responsibility, and nurture personal and communal spiritual growth,

... in which the work of the networks of communication that link diverse peoples, regions, and ways of life is characterized by integrity, respect, and caring,

... in which humankind's most important decisions are based on widely-shared, coherent, and profound understanding of the most critical issues, and

... in which the sacred stories and wisdom of the world's religious and spiritual traditions are broadly disseminated and cherished.

Among the noblest functions of the media (communications, news, entertainment, and education) is the maintenance and expansion of those sinews of community which come from shared access to the central stories and signal events of every era and culture. This building of bridges of communication contributes to the development of a universal human community.

On the occasion of the 1999 Parliament of the World's Religions, convened in Cape Town, South Africa, the Council for a Parliament of the World's Religions calls upon the institution of the media to offer new gifts to the world and its people.

At a time of great challenges and great opportunities, we respectfully ask that individuals, communities, groups, and organizations of the media reassess and redefine their roles in the next century and the next millennium.

We ask that within the world's communications media an urgent and deliberate effort be made to create and implement new modes of creative engagement with religion and the other great institutions whose decisions bear so strongly on the whole of the planetary community. By "creative engagement," we mean the exploration of a new vision of possible futures and the discovery and implementation of new modes of outreach, cooperation, and constructive common action.

A universal consensus on many disputed ethical questions (from bio- and sexual ethics through mass media and scientific ethics, to economic and political ethics) will be difficult to attain.

Nevertheless, even for many controversial questions, suitable solutions should be attainable in the spirit of the fundamental principles we have jointly developed here.

Towards a Global Ethic:
An Initial Declaration

In particular, we ask that within each sector of the institution of communications media the following questions be addressed with the deep care and reflection that can lead to new resolve and new initiative.

1   How might a common statement of ethical standards for media be developed and disseminated—across cultures and disciplines—addressing such issues as socially responsible coverage, a universal professional code, and the commitment to the enrichment of human culture and understanding?

    How can creative engagement with religion assist the media in such an effort?

2   How can a common statement of appropriate methods in media be developed and disseminated—across cultures and disciplines—addressing such issues as rights of privacy, accountability, and self-censorship based on public standards and the common good?

3   How can the media develop liaisons with religious, interreligious, and intercultural groups to broaden understanding of human diversity, to increase coverage of cooperative efforts between religions, and to represent all religions and cultures with respect?

4   How can the media invest most effectively in projects addressing in long-range terms the most critical issues facing the Earth and the human community?

Note: Several members of the Draft Consulting Group have suggested that the list of institutions to which the Call is addressed should be broadened to include Science and the Military. The two sections that follow are offered in response to that suggestion. Please let us know your views. Should either or both be included? If so, why, and, if not, why not?

If either section is included in the Call, what questions should be addressed to the institution in question?

Sample questions are offered in each of the following draft sections.

THE CALL TO SCIENCE

We envision a world

...in which our systems of knowing enhance one another,
...in which our technologies enhance our humanity,
...in which our methods of seeking the truths of existence, rather
than separating us, draw us together, and
...in which we wisely explore the world in which we all live.

Among the noblest functions of science is leading us human beings
out of ourselves toward a world from whose material mysteries we
draw our metaphors and upon whose operating principles we tend
to model our own, as we nurture the life and growth of individuals
and communities.

On the occasion of the 1999 Parliament of the World Religions, convened
in Cape Town, South Africa, the Council for a Parliament of the World's
Religions calls upon the institution of science to offer new gifts to the
world and its people.

At a time of great challenges and great opportunities, we respectfully
ask that individuals, communities, groups, and organizations dedicated
to the advancement of science reassess and redefine their roles in the
next century and the next millennium.

We ask that within the world's scientific community an urgent and
deliberate effort be made to create and implement new modes of creative engagement with religion and the other great institutions whose
decisions bear so strongly on the whole of the planetary community.
By "ìcreative engagement," we mean the exploration of a new vision of
possible futures and the discovery and implementation of new modes
of outreach, cooperation, and constructive common action.

In particular, we ask that within each sector of the institution of science
the following questions be addressed with the deep care and reflection
that can lead to new resolve and new initiative.

In many areas of life a new consciousness of ethical responsibility has already arisen. Therefore we would be pleased if as many professions as possible, such as those of physicians, scientists, business people, journalists, educators, and politicians, would develop up-to-date codes of ethics which would provide specific guidelines for the vexing questions of those particular professions.

Towards a Global Ethic:

An Initial Declaration

**Note: The following questions have been suggested for a possible
Call to Science. What other questions should be offered if this section
is to be included in the final document?**

1   How can science and technology enter into regular dialogue with
    religious and spiritual communities with regard to the framing of
    long-term research programs and the mapping of the long-range
    consequences of scientific and technological innovation?

2   How can science and religion enter into dialogue about the new
    understanding of the origins of the universe that science is now
    shaping?

    Can science's universally sharable account provide new common
    ground on which the world's religions might come together to
    share their own stories in an atmosphere of mutual respect?

3   What are the limits to science? Are there moral/ethical boundaries
    beyond which the scientific enterprise should not go? How can
    these persistent questions best be addressed by science, in dia-
    logue with the other institutions?

THE CALL TO THE MILITARY

We envision a world

... in which the absence of world war becomes a pattern of regional calm and collective good will,

... in which the concept of national security is gradually transformed into the broader ideal of our world as a safe and reassuring place,

... in which weapons of mass destruction no longer determine the paths of our economies or the investments we make in our communities, and

... in which peace is understood as a way of life which must be thoughtfully and lovingly nurtured.

Among the noblest functions of the military is the protection of the freedom, self-determination, and well-being of communities, nations, and peoples through traditions of communal service and collegial purpose.

On the occasion of the 1999 Parliament of the World's Religions, convened in Cape Town, South Africa, the Council for a Parliament of the World's Religions calls upon the institution of the military to offer new gifts to the world and its people.

At a time of great challenges and great opportunities, we respectfully ask that individuals, communities, groups, and organizations of the world's militaries reassess and redefine their roles in the next century and the next millennium.

We ask that within the world's military communities an urgent and deliberate effort be made to create and implement new modes of creative engagement with religion and the other great institutions whose decisions bear so strongly on the whole of the planetary community. By "creative engagement," we mean the exploration of a new vision of possible futures and the discovery and implementation of new modes of outreach, cooperation, and constructive common action.

In particular, we ask that within each sector of the institution of the military the following questions be addressed with the deep care and reflection that can lead to new resolve and new initiative.

**We Declare:
We are interdependent. Each of us depends on the well-being of the whole, and so we have respect for the community of living beings, for people, animals, and plants, and for the preservation of Earth, the air, water, and soil...**

We must treat others as we wish others to treat us. We make a commitment to respect life and dignity, individuality and diversity, so that every person is treated humanely, without exception. We must have patience and acceptance. We must be able to forgive, learning from the past but never allowing ourselves to be enslaved by memories of hate.

Opening our hearts to one another, we must sink our narrow differences for the cause of the world community, practicing a culture of solidarity and relatedness.

Towards a Global Ethic:

An Initial Declaration

Note: The following questions have been suggested for a possible Call to the Military. What other questions should be offered if this section is to be included in the final document?

1 How might the world's religious and spiritual traditions enter into close dialogue with the world's military, together exploring new paths toward peaceful resolution of conflicts?

2 How might the world's religious and spiritual traditions enter into close dialogue with the world's military with respect to the question of the acceptability or unacceptability of the use of arms in the resolution of conflicts, and the criteria (if any) for "just war?"

3 Can and should the military play a central role in conducting an ecological survey of the planet as well as in the development and implementation of a comprehensive plan of stewardship for the Earth?

4 How can the world's military become an institution one of whose primary functions is universal service to humankind in meeting the challenges of natural disasters, famine, and epidemic?

To endorse this Call or for more information, write to:

Council for a Parliament of the World's Religions
P.O. BOX 1630
Chicago, IL 60690-1630
USA

Web site: www.cpwr.org

ENDORSEMENT

As persons reflecting the broad diversity of the Earth's religious, spiritual, cultural, ethnic, and racial communities, we the undersigned join with the Council for a Parliament of the World's Religions in issuing this Call to Our Guiding Institutions.

—We embrace the spirit of this document—

—We applaud its invitation to creative engagement—

—We commit ourselves to the realization of its aims—

—We urge all thoughtful persons to join with us—

SPIRITUAL VALUES IN THE COMMUNITY OF RELIGIONS

Note: It has become quite common to use the terms "spiritual values" and "spirituality," yet there isn't clear agreement about what is meant by them. The words are rich ones, with many connotations that vary depending on who is using them and in what context. Here is one way of understanding spirituality and spiritual values in the context of today's global and pluralistic culture. This summary was written by Brother Wayne Teasdale for the Next Generation program of the Council for a Parliament of the World's Religions. It draws on his scholarship and experience in interfaith dialogue, especially with the contemplative traditions of the world's religions.

The source of spirituality itself is a deep stirring in the human for ultimate meaning, direction and belonging. In its most heightened sense, spirituality is a longing for awareness and experience of the Divine, Boundless Consciousness, or God.

Spirituality and the commitment to spiritual values are always part of a process of growth and transformation in the inner life of the person, but they always have social and practical dimensions as well. These eight key elements can be found in the world's truly mystical and monastic traditions as well as in many religious traditions:

1) an actualized capacity to live morally;
2) a sense of solidarity and community with all life and the earth itself;
3) a deep commitment to non-violence;
4) simplicity of life, expressing itself in a modest lifestyle;
5) self-knowledge;
6) a spiritual practice such as prayer, meditation, contemplation, etc.
7) selfless service and compassionate action, and
8) a prophetic or moral witness and action—the ability and willingness to take risks for justice and the welfare of others, and, in today's context, for the well-being of the planet.

Spirituality also means embracing a commitment to live in the spirit of community among members of the various religions of the world; it requires treating one another with love, compassion, and sensitivity. Spiritual values enable us to stretch or evolve beyond our own self-interest. The fruits of spirituality and spiritual values are courage, moral depth, joy, peace, kindness, mercy, and contemplative wisdom.

Introduction

The objective of the Earth Charter is to set forth an inspiring vision of the fundamental principles of a global partnership for sustainable development and environmental conservation. The Earth Charter Initiative reflects the conviction that a radical change in humanity's attitudes and values is essential to achieve social, economic, and ecological well-being in the twenty-first century. This project is part of the international movement to clarify humanity's shared values and to develop a new global ethics. At it's heart is an expanded sense of community and moral responsibility that embraces all people, future generations, and the larger community of life on Earth. A primary component of the Earth Charter initiative is a process of values internalization by millions of individuals, generating public awareness and the necessary change towards a better future.

For over a decade diverse groups throughout the world have endeavored to create an Earth Charter that would set forth a shared vision of the ethical values and practical guidelines essential to ecological security and sustainable living. In March 1997, at the conclusion of the Rio+5 Forum in Rio de Janeiro, the Earth Charter Commission, which has its Secretariat at the Earth Council in Costa Rica, issued the Benchmark Draft Earth Charter. The Commission also called for ongoing international consultations on the Earth Charter to involve an increasing number of individuals and groups in the process and to improve the text. Based on the many comments and recommendations received from all regions of the world, the Earth Charter Drafting Committee has revised the Charter Preamble and Principles in this Working Draft for Benchmark Draft II and is circulating it for comment. This draft reflects extensive changes, including new principles and subprinciples. The Commission anticipates presenting the official Benchmark Draft II early in 1999, and a final version of the Earth Charter in the year 2000.

One can think of the Earth Charter with its tripartite structure as a Tree of Life. The first three principles are the roots, and the principles in Parts II and III constitute the trunk and the branches. Different groups or local communities can add their own branches.

Adapted from Earth Council documents

The Earth Charter
Working Draft for Benchmark Draft II

Preamble

At this unprecedented time of opportunity and danger, when life on Earth is being placed at risk, it is imperative that we, the People of Earth, declare our independence with and responsibilities to each other, the larger community of life, and the evolving universe. In the midst of a magnificent diversity of cultures and life forms, we are one humanity and one Earth community with a common future.

Planet Earth, our home, is alive with a unique community of life. With reverence for the sources of our being, we give thanks for the gift of life. We affirm that Earth's life support systems and resources are the common heritage of all and a sacred trust. Ensuring a healthy and beautiful Earth with clean air, pure waters, fertile lands, expansive forests, and plentiful oceans is a basic common interest of humanity.

The Earth community stands at a defining moment. With science and technology have come great benefits and also the ability to do great harm. Our patterns of production and consumption are degrading the environment, exhausting resources, and driving whole species to extinction. A dramatic increase in human numbers adds to the pressure on ecological systems. Injustice, inequitable disparities, poverty, lawlessness, and armed conflict deepen the world's suffering. The foundations of global security are threatened. Fundamental changes in our ways of living and relating are necessary.

The choice is ours: to care for Earth and one another or to participate in the destruction of ourselves and the diversity of life. Our priorities must be redefined, building on the work that has already begun. We resolve to find new more just and sustainable ways of balancing self-interest and the common good, diversity and unity, freedom and responsibility, the economy and ecology, the needs of present and of future generations. In the quest for wholeness and happiness, having more is no substitute for being more — expanding ourselves intellectually, aesthetically, ethically, and spiritually.

The securing of human rights for all men and women is the foundation of freedom and justice and a prerequisite to creating socially and ecologically responsible communities. The realization of human rights and the protection of the biosphere are interdependent.

A shared ethical framework that is inclusive and integrated is urgently needed to guide deliberation and decision. Therefore, together in hope, and in solidarity with the community of life, we affirm the following principles and pledge ourselves to work for their implementation through individual, institutional, and collective efforts.

I. GENERAL PRINCIPLES

1. *Respect Earth and all life.*
   a) Recognize the interdependence and intrinsic value of all beings.
   b) Affirm faith in the inherent dignity of all human beings and in the human potential

2. *Care for Earth's community of life in all its diversity.*
   a) Accept the common responsibility to preserve and advance the common good, promoting the well-being of the planet and the whole human family,
   b) Let each individual, group, and nation embrace those distinct responsibilities that are rightfully theirs and that they have the means to fulfill.

The expectation has been that the Earth Charter would draw on the new discoveries and insights of science, the wisdom of the world's religions, and the extensive world literature on global ethics and the ethics of environment and development, as well as international law. It must also reflect what has been learned by those peoples throughout the world whose cultural practices and belief systems effectively promote environmental protection and sustainable living.

Steven C. Rockefeller,

Earth Ethics, *Spring 1997*

3. *Create a global partnership and secure justice, peace, and Earth's abundance and beauty for present and future generations.*
   a) *Design and manage human affairs so that the Earth community as a whole is able to meet its basic needs now and in the future.*
   b) *Be mindful that increased knowledge, power, and freedom bring increased responsibilities.*

II. ECOLOGICAL, ECONOMIC, AND SOCIAL FUNDAMENTALS

4. *Protect and restore the integrity of Earth's ecological systems.*
   a) *Conserve the biodiversity of land and sea, including the genetic diversity within species and the variety of ecosystems.*
   b) *Conserve the ecological processes that sustain and renew life, ensuring the long-term biotic regulation of these processes.*
   c) *Promote the recovery of endangered species and populations, and protect and restore their natural habitats.*
   d) *Establish systems of interconnected nature reserves, including wilderness areas, and other management systems to protect Earth's biodiversity, life support systems, and evolutionary processes.*

5. *Prevent harm to the environment, and when knowledge is limited, err on the side of caution.*
   a) *Stop activities that involve a threat of irreversible or serious harm even when scientific information is incomplete or inconclusive.*
   b) *Give special attention in decision making to the cumulative, long-term, and global consequences of individual and local actions.*
   c) *Recognize that even though attempts to remedy or compensate for harm are necessary, they are not a substitute for prevention.*

6. *Establish and defend the right of all persons to an environment supportive of their dignity, bodily health, and spiritual well-being.*
   a) *Secure the human right to potable water, clean air, uncontaminated soil, and food security.*
   b) *Promote gender equality together with racial, religious, ethnic, and socioeconomic equality as a prerequisite to environmental justice and sustainable human development.*
   c) *Recognize the ignored, protect the vulnerable, and serve those who suffer.*
   d) *Affirm the right of indigenous peoples to their spirituality, knowledge, lands and resources and their related traditional sustainable practices.*

7. *Live sustainably by adopting patterns of consumption, production, and reproduction that respect and safeguard Earth's regenerative capacities, human rights, and community rights.*
   a) *See Part III, Guidelines for Implementing Sustainability.*

8. *Ensure that economic goals and the means of attaining them support and promote human development in an equitable and sustainable manner.*
   a) *Eradicate poverty, generate productive and meaningful employment, strengthen local communities, and improve the quality of life by means of sustainable development.*

b) *Seek to make access to Earth's resources fair and just for all.*

c) *Reduce unnecessary wants and promote the equitable distribution of wealth.*

9. Make the knowledge, values, and skills needed to build just and sustainable communities an integral part of formal education and lifelong learning for all.

a) *Recognize and encourage the contribution of the artistic imagination and the humanities as well as the sciences in environmental education and sustainable development.*

b) *Empower men and women at the local level through education.*

10. Support and establish access to information, inclusive democratic participation in decision making, and transparency, truthfulness, and accountability in governance.

a) *Enable local communities to care for their own environments, and assign responsibilities for environmental protection to the levels of government where they can be carried out effectively.*

b) *Assure the freedom of association and the right to dissent on matters of environmental and social policy.*

c) *Construct systems of world public accountability for transnational corporations, regional and international organizations, and governments.*

11. Practice nonviolence and be an instrument of peace.

a) *Create a culture of peace and cooperation with integrated strategies to prevent violent conflict.*

b) *Recognize that peace is the wholeness created by harmonious and balanced relationships with oneself, other persons, other life, Earth, and the larger whole of which all are a part.*

12. Treat all living beings with compassion, and protect them from cruelty and wanton destruction.

III. GUIDELINES FOR IMPLEMENTING SUSTAINABILITY

13. Do not use renewable resources such as water, soils, forests, grasslands, and fisheries in ways that exceed the regenerative capacity of ecological systems.

14. Eliminate harmful waste and other sources of pollution.

a) *Regard nature as a model, and ensure that any waste material can be either consumed by biological systems or used over the long-term in technical systems.*

b) *Redesign the life cycle of products, reduce the resources used, reuse, and recycle.*

c) *Do not introduce into the air, water, or soil wastes and substances that exceed the assimilation capacity of ecological systems.*

d) *Do not allow concentrations of substances in the environment that endanger the health of human beings and ecosystems.*

15. Act with restraint and efficiency when using energy and rely increasingly on renewable energy sources such as the sun, the wind, and biomass.

16. Advance and put to use knowledge and technologies that facilitate sustainable living and environmental protection.

Questions to explore:

1. Which parts of the Earth Charter reflect your values? Does it challenge any of your beliefs or behaviors?

2. What can religious and spiritual communities learn from others about the Earth Community?

3. Do you hope for "a radical change in humanity's attitudes and values"? What evidence do you see that it is happening—or not?

a) Help to make new ecological knowledge and beneficial technologies available to people throughout the world, strengthening local capacity for sustainability.

17. **Provide, on the basis of gender equality, universal access to health care, and secure the right to sexual and reproductive health, with special concern for women and girls.**

18. **Do not do to the environment of others what you do not want done to your environment.**
    a) Strengthen and enforce international and national law requiring that states take all reasonable measures to prevent activities under their jurisdiction and control from causing transboundary environmental harm.
    b) Prevent transfer of environmentally harmful activities or hazardous materials from one community or nation to another.

19. **Eliminate weapons of mass destruction, promote disarmament, and secure the environment against irreversible or severe damage caused by military activities.**

20. **Create mechanisms and procedures that promote environmentally sound and socially responsible decision making in all sectors of society.**
    a) Adopt local, national, regional, and international sustainability strategies.
    b) Promote interdisciplinary and cross-sectoral collaboration.
    c) Establish market prices and economic indicators that reflect the full environmental and social costs of human activities.
    d) Implement environmental impact assessments.
    e) Create and respect environmental protection standards.
    f) Monitor human environmental impacts and changes in environmental quality.
    g) Share and disseminate information on best practices.

21. **Let the Earth Charter ethic of peace, equity, and prevention of harm govern the exploration and use of orbital and outer space, including the moon and other celestial bodies.**

The creative possibilities before us are great. Our task is the reinvention of industrial-technological civilization and the peaceful management of change. The challenge is ethical and spiritual as well as scientific and technical. A commitment of both minds and hearts is needed. Our best thought and action will flow from the joining of knowledge and compassion.

The engagement of individuals as well as governments is of fundamental importance. The arts, business, the media, the religions, the schools, the sciences, other nongovernmental organizations, and all civil society, including families and youth, have essential roles to play. Progress will require imaginative holistic thinking, a spirit of sharing and mutual support, and a willingness to make sacrifices for the larger good.

Our hope for the future is strengthened by the lives of the many men and women in all nations who in cities, towns, and agricultural communities are leading the way. Embracing the values in this People's Earth Charter, we can grow into a family of diverse cultures and vibrant communities that allows the full potential of all persons to blossom in harmony with the Earth community and the ever-changing universe.

* * *

In order to develop and implement the principles in this Charter, the nations of the world should adopt as a first step an international convention that provides an integrated legal framework for existing and future environmental and sustainable development law and policy.

* * *

A primary component of the Earth Charter initiative is a process of values internalization by millions of individuals, generating public awareness and the necessary change towards a better future.

Religious and Spiritual Contributions to the Earth Charter

The Earth Council's partners and national councils have ensured that the Charter reflects the wisdom and participation of a planet-wide range of religious and spiritual advisors. Among the partners, Global Education Associates engaged its many Roman Catholic and interfaith affiliates in reviewing and contributing to the Charter. The Center for Respect of Life and Environment reached out to numerous governmental, non-governmental, and religious organizations for their contributions, and organized a conference on Spirituality and Sustainability at Assisi, Italy, to encourage dialogue on the charter. The Indigenous People's Network facilitated conferences in San Jose' and prepared recommendations in response to the questions raised in the Charter's report format. The Earth Charter Advisory Group on the Religions engaged more than 250 religious leaders, philosophers, and interfaith groups regarding the document's principles and wording.

According to Dr. Steven C. Rockefeller, coordinator of the Charter's drafting process, there are three reasons for the deliberate outreach to indigenous and religious consultants:

First, it is felt that the Earth Charter can benefit from the wisdom preserved in these traditions; many people would like the Earth Charter to contain an inspiring spiritual vision. Second, without the support of the religions of the world, it will not be possible to change the attitudes, values and behavior of the majority of human beings. Third, unless the world's religions enter into dialogue and collaborate in creating the new global ethics, there is little chance of creating peace on Earth and achieving development and environmental conservation.

Earth Ethics, Winter/Spring 1997

Additional information is available from: Earth Charter Consultation, The Earth Council, Apdo. 2323-1002, San Jose', COSTA RICA or on the Earth Charter web site (www.earthcharter.org).

WORLD FAITHS AND DEVELOPMENT

Closing Statement, issued by Dr. George Carey, Archbishop of Canterbury, and Mr. James Wolfensohn, President of The World Bank, on behalf of representatives of the nine major world religions that gathered for the World Faiths and Development Dialogue on February 18-19, 1998, at Lambeth Palace, London.

1. This has been a precious opportunity for frank and intensive dialogue between religious leaders and development experts drawn from nine of the world's religious faiths, and leading staff of the World Bank. We are profoundly grateful to all the participants. What has drawn us together is a deep moral concern for the future of human well-being and dignity. We cannot accept the suffering of so many millions of people around the world.

2. We are strengthened in our conviction that the definition and practice of desirable development must have regard to spiritual, ethical, environmental, cultural and social considerations, if it is to be sustainable and contribute to the well-being of all, especially the poorest and weakest members of society.

3. All participants in the Dialogue agreed that "well-being" must imply the elimination of the suffering caused by absolute material poverty whilst also recognizing the importance of spiritual and cultural life. Our understanding of poverty and development has been widened and enriched by the exchange between the World Bank experts and the different faiths with their diverse interpretations of what it means to lead a fully human life.

4. We believe that this dialogue has contributed to a deepening of the religious communities' understanding of how much benefit there is in being part of a discussion with such a wide circle of people working on development issues, and in particular having the opportunity to hear from people engaged from different perspectives, both religious and secular. It can only be in such a context of listening and speaking that real changes can be forthcoming. The challenge to all of us is how to pool our talents to overcome poverty as it has become defined for us through our discussions. We are particularly keen to start some more small scale and practical activities, which could act as models for future development.

5. We have achieved an important consensus on the need for the World Bank and major religious communities to continue and develop this dialogue, to deepen our relationship with one another and to look forward to possible new ways of working together in the future at many different levels.

Outcome

6. For example, the religious communities will be invited to influence the thinking of the World Bank by participating in the studies and discussions embodied in the Bank's annual World Development Reports. This will be particularly appropriate and timely in relation to the year 2000 Report on Understanding Poverty.

7. We shall establish joint working groups to explore together themes of concern such as: community building; hunger and food security; environmental sustainability; preservation of cultural heritage (including sacred sites); violence and post-conflict reconstruction; education; and social service delivery, and we shall look at areas of joint research to further the analytical dialogue initiated by our discussion on criteria.

8. The Bank desires to improve its staff's understanding of the main beliefs and contributions of the different religions of the countries in which they are working and will invite the participation of representatives from the world's faiths in Bank staff training programmes. Similarly, the religious communities wish to deepen their understanding of international development issues and the Bank will seek to help in this regard.

9. The religious communities already contribute substantially to the design and implementation of several development programmes, significantly improving their effectiveness. We hope they will feel encouraged to explore further opportunities for partnership in this field, both bilaterally and on a multi-faith basis. We encourage the stimulation of pilot projects to develop good practice at the initiative of the countries themselves and with the collaboration of the religious communities and with the full backing of the Bank.

10. A light and flexible steering group will monitor and facilitate progress in these areas as well as preparing the future development of this work. They will oversee the publication of papers relating to this Dialogue.

11. We invite religious faith communities, international agencies and governments throughout the world to support and participate in this continuing drive for better understanding between development agencies and world faiths in defining and delivering development programmes. We believe this will help improve the long-term well-being of all the world's people and safeguard the spiritual, moral, environmental and cultural resources on which they depend.

Questions to explore:

1. What is the appropriate place of spiritual and religious ethical standards in defining the goals and methods of material development?

2. How can religious or interreligious groups serve a higher common ground among the agendas of banks, corporations, and governments?

3. Can a market economy that promotes consumerism and builds on the individual's desire for material gain be reconciled with sustainable ways of life?

*   *   *

What Is Significant about this Statement and Dialogue?

Archbishop George Carey, head of the world-wide Anglican Communion and host, said it was the "most remarkable meeting in the 800-year history of Lambeth Palace", because it brought together high-level religious and spiritual leaders from many faiths to meet formally with leaders of the World Bank, a secular agency of the UN. Participants came from nine faiths, including main traditions within the following: Baha'i, Buddhist, Christian, Hindu, Jain, Muslim, Sikh and Tao.

In recent years, the Bank has been reassessing its approach to development. This rethinking by the world's largest development funding agency has come partly in response to criticism that World Bank projects are disconnected from the needs of local communities. The Dialogue that led to the above Statement represents a formal step in the Bank's consultations with religious leaders. Its significance is that religious and spiritual values are emerging as factors in the assessment of projects, even in the secular worlds of finance and economic development.

Responses by participants support Dr. Carey's assessment. "For the first time in contemporary economics," said Martin Palmer, director of the International Consultancy on Religion, Education and Culture, "the role of religion in development was not just publicly acknowledged or even acclaimed, but brought into a partnership with one of the largest and, some would argue, most vociferously secular organizations in the world." Mr. Wolfensohn, President of the World Bank, noted in a closing statement: "What is clear is that what has come out of this meeting is that there is a unity between us—a unity of the concern for physical livelihood but also spiritual and cultural continuity." (*One Country,* the Newsletter of the International Baha'i Community, Jan./March, 1998).

"The significance of the meeting is not to be underestimated," said Swami Vibudhesha Teertha, one of the Hindu representatives. **"This dialogue redefined poverty, prosperity and progress."**

One Country,
Jan./March 1998

Prominent Buddhist author and participant Sulak Sivaraksa noted that

> *I was not hopeful before the meeting as I thought that the World Bank only wanted us to become their decorations, that is, to show to the world that they care for world religions and cultures. However, having been together at Lambeth Palace, I feel that Dr. Wolfensohn was sincere and I hope that he will be successful . . . and that the World Bank will serve the poor and oppressed, listen to them and try to help with skillful means to overcome the obstacles put forward by their own governments and corrupted politicians [as well as by the] multinational corporations."* (*Seeds of Peace,* May–Sept. 1998)

PROMOTING A CULTURE OF PEACE

In recent years, the United Nations Educational, Scientific, and Cultural Organization (UNESCO) has taken new interest in the role of religions, churches, and spiritual communities in promoting a culture of peace. UNESCO's founding document includes reflections on peace as the purpose of the United Nations: "Since wars are born in the minds of men, it is in the minds of men that the bastions of peace must be built." A series of conferences with religious and spiritual leaders and scholars, sponsored by UNESCO since 1993, has noted the varying roles that religions may play in conflictive situations as well as in creating a culture of peace. The following statement was issued by the 1994 meeting.

Declaration on the Role of Religion in the Promotion of a Culture of Peace

We, participants in the meeting, "The Contribution by Religions to the Culture of Peace," organized by UNESCO and the Centre UNESCO de Catalunya, which took place in Barcelona from 12 to 18 December, 1994,

Deeply concerned with the present situation of the world, such as increasing armed conflicts and violence, poverty, social injustice, and structures of oppression;

Recognizing that religion is important in human life;

DECLARE:

Our World

1. We live in a world in which isolation is no longer possible. We live in a time of unprecedented mobility of peoples and intermingling of cultures. We are all interdependent and share an inescapable responsibility for the well-being of the entire world.

2. We face a crisis which could bring about the suicide of the human species or bring us a new awakening and a new hope. We believe that peace is possible. We know that religion is not the sole remedy for all the ills of humanity, but it has an indispensable role to play in this most critical time.

Looking at international problems, it is easy to find religious components in existing wars and conflicts. Religions are often used to legitimate the ideological, economic or political interests which are the most immediate cause of conflicts.

But religions can be of great help in the creation of a culture of peace that would make it possible to prevent conflicts, defuse violence and build structures that are fairer and freer. . . .

Programme for the 1993 UNESCO conference

Religions can remind us of fundamental aspects of human dignity, of openness to others, of the real priorities in individual lives and the lives of all peoples.

Religions can encourage us on the paths of generosity and cooperation. Religion is a great source for insight and ethical courage. . . .

Religions can always take the side of justice, nonviolence, and peace. They can do so because they love truth, are free and have a great spiritual strength.

from Programmes for the 1993 and 1994 UNESCO conferences

3. We are aware of the world's cultural and religious diversity. Each culture represents a universe in itself and yet it is not closed. Cultures give religions their language, and religions offer ultimate meaning to each culture. Unless we recognize pluralism and respect diversity, no peace is possible. We strive for the harmony which is at the very core of peace.

4. We understand that culture is a way of seeing the world and living in it. It also means the cultivation of those values and forms of life which reflect the world-views of each culture. Therefore neither the meaning of peace nor of religion can be reduced to a single and rigid concept, just as the range of human experience cannot be conveyed by a single language.

5. For some cultures, religion is a way of life, permeating every human activity. For others it represents the highest aspirations of human existence. In still others, religions are institutions that claim to carry a message of salvation.

6. Religions have contributed to the peace of the world, but they have also led to division, hatred, and war. Religious people have too often betrayed the high ideals they themselves have preached. We feel obliged to call for sincere acts of repentance and mutual forgiveness, both personally and collectively, to one another, to humanity in general, and to Earth and all living beings.

Peace

7. Peace implies that love, compassion, human dignity, and justice are fully preserved.

8. Peace entails that we understand that we are all interdependent and related to one another. We are all individually and collectively responsible for the common good, including the well-being of future generations.

9. Peace demands that we respect Earth and all forms of life, especially human life. Our ethical awareness requires setting limits to technology. We should direct our efforts towards eliminating consumerism and improving the quality of life.

10. Peace is a journey—a never-ending process.

Commitment

11. We must be at peace with ourselves; we strive to achieve inner peace through personal reflection and spiritual growth, and to cultivate a spirituality which manifests itself in action.

12. We commit ourselves to support and strengthen the home and family as the nursery of peace.

In homes and families, communities, nations and the world:

13. We commit ourselves to resolve or transform conflicts without using violence, and to prevent them through education and the pursuit of justice.

14. We commit ourselves to work towards a reduction in the scandalous economic differences between human groups and other forms of violence and threats to peace, such as waste of resources, extreme poverty, racism, all types of terrorism, lack of caring, corruption, and crime.

15. We commit ourselves to overcome all forms of discrimination, colonialism, exploitation, and domination and to promote institutions based on shared responsibility and participation. Human rights, including religious freedom and the rights of minorities, must be respected.

16. We commit ourselves to assure a truly humane education for all. We emphasize education for peace, freedom, and human rights, and religious education to promote openness and tolerance.

17. We commit ourselves to a civil society which respects environmental and social justice. This process begins locally and continues to national and transnational levels.

18. We commit ourselves to work towards a world without weapons and to dismantle the industry of war.

Questions to explore:

1. **What is the common perception of the role of religions in situations of conflict and crisis? Is it an accurate perception?**

2. **Should "promoting a culture of peace" be a top priority for religious and spiritual communities?**

3. **Should religion ever be used to support political, social or economic agendas that involve the use of violence?**

Religious Responsibility

19. Our communities of faith have a responsibility to encourage conduct imbued with wisdom, compassion, sharing, charity, solidarity, and love; inspiring one and all to choose the path of freedom and responsibility. Religions must be a source of helpful energy.

20. We will remain mindful that our religions must not identify themselves with political, economic, or social powers, so as to remain free to work for justice and peace. We will not forget that confessional political regimes may do serious harm to religious values as well as to society. We should distinguish fanaticism from religious zeal.

21. We will favor peace by countering the tendencies of individuals and communities to assume or even to teach that they are inherently superior to others. We recognize and praise the nonviolent peacemakers. We disown killing in the name of religion.

22. We will promote dialogue and harmony between and within religions, recognizing and respecting the search for truth and wisdom that is outside our religion. We will establish dialogue with all, striving for a sincere fellowship on our earthly pilgrimage.

Appeal

23. Grounded in our faith, we will build a culture of peace based on nonviolence, tolerance, dialogue, mutual understanding, and justice. We call upon the institutions of our civil society, the United Nations system, governments, governmental and non-governmental organizations, corporations, and the mass media, to strengthen their commitments to peace and to listen to the cries of the victims and the dispossessed. We call upon the different religious and cultural traditions to join hands together in this effort, and to cooperate with us in spreading the message of peace.